the BIG picture

the BIG picture

An Honest Examination of
God, Science, and Purpose

P. D. Hemsley

eLectio Publishing
Little Elm, TX
www.eLectioPublishing.com

Dedication:

To my wife Cathy, who has been with me through thick and thin for over 30 years, and to my daughters Lizzy and Becky who both outsmart me.

Foreword

Scientific discovery has brought material benefits and physical comfort to mankind. The predictability of matter leads us to assume that it behaves according to fixed laws, and this belief has led engineers to develop tools and machinery to manipulate the environment, doctors to develop cures for many diseases, and farmers to grow crops with greatly increased yields. Many of the scourges of previous times have been overcome leading, in the Western world at least, to longer lifetimes and better health. However, this has also led to the belief that everything is predictable and controllable. If anything goes wrong (by which we mean it causes us distress or discomfort) then it must be fixable, and if it hasn't been fixed it must be someone else's fault.

Personal rights have grown, but personal responsibility has diminished. Laws to protect the weak have bred the belief that it is the state's job and not our individual duty to help out those less fortunate than ourselves. Mechanisation that was supposed to give more leisure time has led to lost jobs and loss of purpose. Competition and the shrinking of the geographical world has meant that there is someone, somewhere who will work harder or longer hours than we do, and the pressure grows to produce more for less. The availability of loans means that goods can be obtained now if we promise to pay later. To pay the loan we need a job. Fear of job loss drives us to work longer hours and accept less pay. The purpose of life becomes to produce. The mechanism which fuels demand and production is the economy. The economy becomes the measure of the health of a nation.

Is that what it's all about?

Is my value simply what I can produce?

Am I measured just by what I can earn?

If I retain the worldview that the economy is king then the implication is yes, but that doesn't feel right. I want to be valued and loved as a person. I want a worldview that speaks to my heart and my mind and not just my wallet, and I want it to be based on sound thinking and evidence.

Science has brought great technological and medical benefits to mankind; cars, televisions, fridges, telephones, electricity and so on. But science has also brought guns and bullets, pollution, global drug trafficking and job losses. Science seems to dominate my life, telling me what I should or shouldn't do to keep healthy, avoid risk and live longer, but it doesn't tell me why I would want to live longer. Science doesn't give any purpose to my life.

Religion offers purpose, but it too seems to want to control me and dominate me. Religion has been used as justification for many great atrocities: the Spanish Inquisition, child sacrifices, the Crusades. Religious people seem to want to tell me how to behave, and to judge and criticise me, claiming to represent the will of God.

I want to know the truth. I want to know what science can tell me about how the universe works, and perhaps where I came from. I want the benefits that science can bring, but not at the cost of becoming a slave to its dictates. I want to know why I am here, what my purpose in life is, or even if there is one. If there is a God I want to know what He thinks. I want the benefit of knowing that I have a purpose, but not at the cost of becoming a slave to rules from another human being.

And so I investigate, weigh up evidence in all forms and seek a holistic worldview that works. I have explored what we know from the physical and biological sciences, and I have researched historical evidence for God. I have tested what is actually known, and what is speculation, extrapolation or personal opinion and rhetoric.

This book presents my conclusions, and some of the evidence that brought me to draw them. I offer what I believe is a consistent, healthy and constructive worldview based on sound evidence. I've called it Minimalist Christianity. Whether you agree with my conclusion or not, I hope that many of the myths that currently inhibit so many of us will have been weakened or dispelled. I hope that a step can be taken towards finding purpose and experiencing life in abundance.

Contents

Introduction

Don't you just hate it when someone won't listen? They read an article in the newspaper and are immediately an expert on a subject. They won't listen to the facts. Their mind is made up.

But perhaps we are all the same. We have a little information and we think we know it all. Or our favourite celebrity says something that we agree with and it confirms us in our opinion. We never really bother to check out the facts for ourselves.

A few years ago I decided to dig deeper into questions of science, God and philosophy to try to get to the facts. Were the Creationists right, and is evolution an evil myth? Were the scientists right and is there no need for God? Are we deluded if we think we have free will? Can miracles happen? Did Jesus exist, and if so was he just a good moral teacher? What is it that makes me "me?"

It is impossible to gather all the information that there is, but I think I have enough to justify some conclusions. And those conclusions are what this book is about. I discuss each conclusion in a separate section of the book. You can read them all in one go, or one at a time. You can choose to agree or disagree, but your choice will be based on deeper evidence than the popular press might provide. I challenge you to open your mind to the possibilities that the evidence suggests. Be ready to slaughter some sacred cows, and enjoy the taste of the barbequed beef.

So here are my conclusions that I will explore in the following chapters:

- Everyone relies on faith.
- Science describes an incredible universe.
- The universe exhibits design and purpose.
- Not everything can be explained by science
- Reason leads to a sound definition of God
- Jesus lived and spoke for God.
- God has a purpose for each of us

And the final chapter describes what it looks like to live in the light of my conclusions:

The Way of the Minimalist Christian

Almost all books in the arena of science and faith are hostile and adversarial. The authors set up straw men of their opponent's arguments, dismantle them and then preach their own arguments to their disciples. Such books are written for those who already agree with the point of view of the author and want to be told how weak the arguments against their views are. As such, many adopt an extreme and uncompromising position.

Logical fallacy: Straw man

The person using the straw man fallacy argues a case by presenting a false and often simplified version of the opponent's argument and then easily knocks it down. This fallacy can be surprisingly common particularly in discussions about the existence or otherwise of God.

The neutral reader is forced either to take sides or dismiss the whole argument as irrelevant and simply get on with his daily life.

In contrast, this is a book of information and reason. I have tried to present information and arguments in a balanced and gracious manner that allows you to consider the big questions of life without feeling bludgeoned to adopt my opinion. You don't need to be familiar with the subject matter to degree level; the science, philosophy and religion are explained in a straightforward manner.

I recognise that there are intelligent atheists and intelligent believers in God, and in the end there is always a case for whatever someone wants to believe. The reader is therefore treated with respect. However, I consider how we might have formed our beliefs and how we actually know anything. I have listed in an appendix and interspersed in the text a number of common logical fallacies to highlight underhand tactics that are often used to convince the unwary through manipulation of emotions or fallacious thinking.

The book explores and presents evidence from science and history, and from ancient thinkers. It considers what we might mean by "God," describes current scientific knowledge and discusses what science tells us about God. The book also highlights areas where science and the laws of physics struggle to provide an adequate explanation for known facts.

Over the centuries, many have claimed to speak for God and thereby gained powerful positions. In contrast, Jesus claimed to be one with God and was killed as a result. The book examines the historical evidence for Jesus, and the context and content of the Gospel documents.

The book concludes by describing a response to the evidence put forward throughout the book. My response, Minimalist Christianity, focuses on simply following the teaching of Jesus, pursuing goodness and wholeness, and loving others. It distances itself from two millennia of religious dogma and intolerance that have made Christianity unattractive in the eyes of many.

Let's begin!

Chapter 1: Everyone Relies on Faith

*Slartibartfast, "Perhaps I'm old and tired, but I think
that the chances of finding out what's actually going
on are so absurdly remote that the only thing to do is
to say, 'Hang the sense of it,' and keep yourself busy.
I'd much rather be happy than right any day."
Arthur Dent, "And are you?"
Slartibartfast, "Ah, no. Well, that's where it all falls
down, of course."
(Hitchhikers Guide to the Galaxy by Douglas
Adams)[1]*

I imagine that many of us are like Slartibartfast, keeping
ourselves busy and hoping for happiness. Yet how many of us would
claim that we have really got everything sorted? Do we empathise
with *"Ah, no. Well, that's where it all falls down, of course."*

There are times when we decide that we really need to get to
grips with what's going on, to think afresh about what life is all
about. So we want to find out the truth, to understand the big picture
and where we fit in it. How are we going to go about it?

We could experiment and see what works, but that probably
got us in the state we are in, so we need something more thorough.
We hear so many different messages, from the media, from science,
from the many different religious leaders, from politicians that we
might decide that we will only change if something has been
rigorously proven to work—but then we have to define rigorous.
And unfortunately (or perhaps fortunately, as it gives us a choice)
nothing that affects our outlook on life can be rigorously proven, in
the end we all act on faith. When we were young, we were open to
all ideas; we hadn't yet been indoctrinated with the dogmas of the

---

[1] Douglas Adams: *Hitchhiker's Guide to the Galaxy* ISBN 978-3320258641

day. But once we've been trained how to think like those around us we become more set in our ways and so we tend to ask for proof before we are willing to change. Perhaps the time has come to regain the boldness of our childhood?

Am I Open Minded?

So as we start out let me ask the question, "Am I open minded, ready to follow where evidence leads, with no preconceptions?"

Now I'm sure you've answered "yes" because none of us would like to admit otherwise, but actually, it may be impossible to start <u>any</u> investigation without preconceptions. They are the motivation behind many investigations . . . the desire to obtain proof of what we already think about something.

Preconceptions are almost inherent in the scientific approach—we think of a theory, and then we investigate to test it. If we are honest, we will admit that we like our theories and feel good when they are proved right.

Perhaps there is one preconception that I will allow at this stage; that each one of us matters. I matter. You matter. Our friends and neighbours all matter. If we don't matter then there is no point in anything and it's best not to think any deeper. That road leads to despair.

If we are going to explore these questions fully we are going to have to consider questions of God, science, reason, history and more. We are going to have to include objective data and subjective experience; objectivity keeps us from being deluded but it is the subjective that really matters to us.

Even if we try to think about an issue with an open mind, we nevertheless carry many assumptions that we don't realise. Speaking personally, my scientific education and engineering career have both instilled a basic assumption of materialism: the fabric of the universe is all there is. When people talk about a spiritual dimension, is it just another material dimension that we can't see? And if there is a

6

spiritual dimension, how can it interact with the physical universe? Or if there isn't a separate spiritual dimension then where does God exist? These are not straightforward questions, but I've come to realise that they are valid. I have had to challenge a lot of what I took simply as common sense and to open my mind to new possibilities.

It can be difficult to refresh our way of thinking, particularly if we are surrounded by others who have a similar outlook to ourselves. In a recent discussion on European history with a university student he mentioned that such and such country was fascist. It led me to ask what it is that makes the people there fascist. Is it genetically programmed into each individual there? If you took any one of them and brought them up elsewhere would they be fascist? I think it likely that they wouldn't. They are fascist because everyone around them is fascist. They are unconsciously trained to be fascists.

> **Logical fallacy: Hypothesis contrary to fact**
>
> One can look at this as speculation, or sometimes wishful thinking. If "this" hadn't happened then "that" would have happened, or "this" only happened because of "that." For example, "If I'd married someone else then I'd be happier."

So what are we doing in our country? What are we training ourselves to think like? What assumptions do we hold, and are they valid? Books such as *The Science Delusion* by Rupert Sheldrake[2] challenge many of the assumptions of the day. He asks us to challenge our scientific dogmas, our blind assumptions. Even if we end up thinking the same as we did before, we have a more solid basis for our beliefs if we go through the process of challenging our assumptions.

---

[2] Rupert Sheldrake: *The Science Delusion* ISBN 978-1444727944

Implications

Whenever anyone is presenting a case we might ask ourselves, "If I were to accept what is being presented and agree with the author, what would be the implications for me? How willing would I be to accept those implications? Do I need to understand the implications before I start?"

Many parents choose not to have their babies tested for Down's syndrome because they would not be willing to accept a termination of the pregnancy and so feel that there is no point in knowing before the child is born. Others might need to understand all the implications before deciding; how accurate is the test, and what are the options available if the child tests positive? Still others might insist that they must have the test because they are not prepared to risk having a child with Down's syndrome and would terminate the pregnancy if that were shown to be likely by the test.

This is a book that deals with questions of God. This may worry some people. If they were to be convinced that God is real they would have to become the sort of bigoted judgemental fanatic that represents the worst face of religion. They may think that they would need to join a religion and accept all that they are told without thinking, and be associated with all the religious atrocities of the past. Or that they will have to give up their Sunday morning lie-in and trot off to church with a bunch of hypocrites. If these thoughts resonate with you, take courage—it doesn't have to be like that.

Logical Fallacy: Slippery slope

The "slippery slope" fallacy implies that an action will lead to a sequence of events ending in disaster, and that therefore the action mustn't me taken.

For example: "If you believe in God you might become a religious fundamentalist. Religious fundamentalists flew into the twin towers so you shouldn't believe in God."

Fear

People can be frightened by the prospect of change, but often change is beneficial. For instance, when redundancies are announced, there is a lot of fear in the workforce. Some may have been in the same job for thirty years, and they simply don't know anything else—how will they cope if they have to find another job? And yet being forced to change jobs can be a most liberating and life-changing experience. I recall hearing a report that those who remain behind after a round of redundancies are likely to be more stressed than those who have been made redundant. They are still in the same job, but with increased fear of losing it and still in fear of change, whereas those who have left are now busy rebuilding their new lives and careers. That's not to say it's easy to change, but a change in a job or a worldview can be very liberating.

Peer Pressure

Perhaps we don't want to change our views because of what others might think of us. We've probably aired our opinions sufficiently to our friends that any major change would be an embarrassment. Or perhaps we live or work in a culture where there is only one accepted way of thinking. We might find that we have to live a double life, adopting one attitude at work and another in private. For instance, to progress a career as a scientist it is necessary to publish papers and learned articles. Such articles are subject to peer review. This process is in place to ensure that sound scientific information is published and that mistakes do not get propagated. But the process inherently risks that only those papers that conform to the present scientific way of thinking are published. If a scientist becomes too free thinking, then the peer review process may prevent his papers being published and his career may come to a grinding halt. Reputation is essential, and doing anything that might lose it is risky.

An ambitious scientist may be fearful of embracing religion. Religion allows that God might interfere with the workings of the world. That might mean that the universe is not completely

Logical fallacy: Ad Populum

This is an appeal to our basic desire to fit in with the crowd. I have seen heated discussions about how many scientists believe in God. The answer is of no relevance to the question of whether God exists or not. The reason behind the numbers might be relevant, but the numbers themselves are of no consequence.

predictable, which would seem to undermine the basis of all the work of science. Allowing the existence of God might mean that it will be impossible to have a complete scientific theory that predicts everything—which is challenging to anyone who invests their life in seeking it.

Similarly, in religious circles it can be damaging not only to one's career but also to one's life to challenge the current way of thinking. Men and women have been labelled heretics and have been burnt at the stake for holding different religious beliefs.

Religious people may have a deep fear of science. Apart from the vocal assertions made by some atheists that science has done away with God, there can be fear that science might undermine or even disprove certain traditions or beliefs that the given religion may hold dear, or even sacred. A religious man may have invested so much in his religion that he's lost the desire, and maybe even the ability, to be open to learning that some of what he's been taught is incorrect. Yet surely a truly godly man would be desperate to be corrected if he were misunderstanding God? In her book *Awesome God*, Sara Maitland encourages religious people to embrace what can be learned from science:

> *Start with "God exists" and everything we can learn*
> *will tell us more about God.*[3]

---

[3] Sara Maitland: *Awesome God: Creation, Commitment and Joy* ISBN: 978-0281054190

So returning to the question, "Am I open minded, ready to follow where evidence leads, with no preconceptions?" we can see that it is almost impossible not to have preconceptions or preconditions. A first step in challenging them is to consider how we came to believe them in the first place. How did we come to really know what we know?

How Do We Know Anything?

There is truth and there is what we believe. Some things are true, but we don't believe them. Some things we believe, but they are not true. Only when something is true and we believe it does it become knowledge. Now whilst that is fine philosophically, how do we know that something is true? I would contend that we can never know that anything is true; we can only believe it to be true. So let's explore how we might come to believe something to be true.

The first way we get to know anything is when someone tells us. Initially we trust everything our parents tell us, but at some stage when we are young, we learn about lies. We learn that something that we have been told is not true. We found out that Father Christmas is not real. I remember when I was young, my brother told me something must be true because it was written in a book. Little did I realise—yet we still tend to believe what we read. If something is in the newspaper our inclination is to believe it, particularly if it supports a previously held opinion. There have been a few instances where I was fully aware of the facts about an event reported in the newspapers, and it was astonishing to see the glaring mistakes in what was reported, and to see how people's words were misquoted.

So we learn scepticism and we learn that we can be misled, but nevertheless we still tend to believe most of what we are told. Believing something only because we are told it is an act of faith, and most, if not all knowledge starts that way.

Testing for Truth

As we learn to be more sceptical, we might want to check something out before we actually believe it. We might compare what we been told with our own experiences, observations or understanding. We might compare with other things we've been told. We might research in books or on the Internet to see if the supposed fact is corroborated or if there are other opinions or explanations. We will check it against our worldview and see if it fits. We can check out quantitative statements with our understanding of mathematics, statistics or scientific theory. If it passes these tests, the information moves towards us considering that we know it to be true.

We might decide to act on something that we've been told is true: to experiment and see if the results of our experiment match what we have been told will happen. If they do, we are more likely to consider what we have been told is true.

In dealing with questions of God, once again we may draw on experiment, on what we are told and on our personal experience. Sometimes what we are told comes from a holy text, the Bible for instance, and so we need to decide on the provenance or authorship of the holy text to decide how far we can trust it. If we think that it was written by God, or by an eyewitness to an event then we will trust the details far more than if we think it was written hundreds of years after the event by someone with an agenda.

If we think about what it means to know something in the field of science, it often comes down to some sort of principle or law. There are mathematical and scientific laws such as $2 + 2 = 4$. We know that $E=MC^2$. We know that heat won't flow from cold to hot. We might know these to be absolute truths, but even here we are still acting in faith that the laws are correct, and indeed that the universe behaves according to fixed laws. So we don't *really* know.

We live according to moral principles or laws; we know that it is wrong to murder, or steal. But in the field of morality it is difficult to determine if there is an absolute truth. It depends on what the question is and what the circumstances are. For example, John stabs Jane with a needle. Was he wrong to do so? What if he is giving an injection? At what point does pain or discomfort constitute suffering? Is suffering always a bad thing?

I believe that there are some basic absolute truths. It is always right to love others. (I'm not of course talking about sexual love / lust). It is always right to desire the best for others, and to exert oneself for their wellbeing.

Truth That We Can't Prove

We often consider mathematics to be absolute and pure truth. We believe this because we all know that one potato and another potato make two potatoes. And since we can understand this simple mathematical equation to be absolutely true we might extrapolate that all mathematical theorems are absolutely true and provable.

Surprisingly Austrian mathematician Kurt Gödel developed two theorems of mathematical logic that proved that at least some mathematics is un-provable; that it has to be taken on faith.

John Lennox (another mathematician) describes that

> *If arithmetic is consistent then that fact is one of the things that cannot be proved in the system. It is something that we can only believe on the basis of the evidence, or by appeal to higher axioms. This has been succinctly summarised by saying that if a religion is something whose foundations are based on faith, then mathematics is the only religion that can prove it is a religion!*[4]

In effect Gödel's first theorem is saying that although we know that one potato and another potato are two potatoes, it cannot be proved mathematically and so has to be taken on faith.

Deception

Whilst we have to take most of what we are told on faith we begin to trust that they are correct if we hear them from a number of sources, or from a source which gave us other information that we found to be correct.

---

[4] John C. Lennox: *God's Undertaker – Has Science Buried God?* ISBN 978-0-7459-5371-7

Some authors use this approach to lead people to believe things that are not true. An author can cleverly intertwine fact with fiction, and so readers can be misled about what is truth and what is not. Dan Brown uses this to great effect in his novels. He includes many details that people know are correct, and refers to events which they have heard about but don't know the details about. And then he makes up details and supposedly hidden secrets which the reader begins to believe to be true.

Such techniques are excellent for storytelling, interspersing some known facts in the fiction makes the story come to life and be more believable. The reader enjoys it, the author sells more books, but it does mislead. At the start of Brown's book *The Da Vinci Code*[5] he writes:

FACT:

The Vatican prelature known as Opus Dei is a deeply devout Catholic sect that has been the topic of recent controversy due to reports of brainwashing. . . . Opus Dei *has just completed construction of a $47 million National Headquarters . . .*

Looking carefully, the sentence does not claim as fact that there has been brainwashing, but simply that there has been a "controversy" due to "reports of brainwashing'. The construction of a new building is irrelevant. Yet the unwary reader will be left with the impression that Opus Dei is a corrupt organisation that brainwashes its members to pay for an expensive headquarters.

So how are you to know if anything written in this book is correct? Maybe you will take it on trust. Maybe you will follow up some of the sections, check them out in other books or literature, or research the Internet. Maybe you'll even do some calculations. If you find some facts to be accurate you might accept others without checking, or you might decide to check up on them all. All are valid approaches.

---

5 Dan Brown: *The Da Vinci Code* – ISBN 978-0752100401

Logical Fallacies

People can hold very strong views on questions of life. The means of exploring the truth can often be very adversarial; the goal seems to be to win the argument rather than to reach the truth. Proponents on either side of an argument often use fallacious rhetoric when presenting their case. Fallacious arguments are common simply because they can be very effective. Although they contain incorrect reasoning they often affect our feelings and distract us from clear thinking.

We must be careful not to dismiss an argument *because* it is a logical fallacy. Something may be factually correct even if it is not correctly reasoned. But it's as well to be alert to some of the more common fallacies.

Unclear Definitions

A second thing to be wary of is unclear definition of words or concepts. We use many words so loosely that when questioned we can find it hard to know precisely what we mean by them. People sometimes use language like "evolution caused the giraffe to have a long neck," yet I'm sure that different people have a very different understanding of what the term "evolution" means. Even the term "God" has many different meanings or interpretations; is everyone talking about the same thing? I find that it can be helpful in discussions to ask the simple question "What do you mean by . . . ?" because unless I know what the other person is talking about, how can I understand their point?

Superficial Explanations

Sometimes people hear a brief news report, and immediately jump to conclusions about the full picture behind the story, usually based on their own preconceptions or prejudices. The consequences can be serious. Atheist biologist Steve Jones once commented that some Muslim biology students were walking out of his lectures, saying that their motive was that the course material was incompatible with their Creationist beliefs. The story was picked up by the Daily Mail[6]. Other newspapers and other celebrities offered quotes: Richard Dawkins commented to the Times Educational Supplement that. *"I think there's a very, very pernicious influence that is lasting up to the university years."*[7] The story then appears on websites such as *Jihadwatch*. The website contains a string of abusive

> **Logical fallacy: Missing the point**
>
> When evidence implies a conclusion, but the conclusion that is drawn is not the correct conclusion, or is extrapolating beyond the conclusion that can be drawn. For example, "I have seen Tom leaving his house on foot every day, so I know that he walks to work." Whilst it is correct that Tom walks part of the way to work, it is not correct to conclude that he walks all the way to work.

---

[6]Mail Online 28th Nov 2011 - http://www.dailymail.co.uk/news/article-2066795/Muslim-students-walking-lectures-Darwinism-clashes-Koran.html accessed 23/2/13

[7]http://www.telegraph.co.uk/news/religion/8814298/Richard-Dawkins-attacks-Muslim-schools-for-stuffing-childrens-minds-with-alien-rubbish.html accessed 25/2/13

comments about Muslims, for example: *"In fact they don't need any infidel science, only the Qur'an, and should refuse all higher education in the West. Better yet these Muslims should be strongly encouraged to take off for the Islamic enlightened deserts of the Middle East. Morons."* [8]

> **Logical fallacy: The Fallacy fallacy**
>
> A logical fallacy is a mistake in reasoning, but to commit a logical fallacy doesn't mean that the case being argued is incorrect. The facts being argued may be correct but the case is being made with poor reasoning.

Absolutely every responder "fills in the blanks" in the story and launches into "us and them" abuse, based on their own preconceptions. A hasty comment or misleading report can spread rapidly and fuel existing prejudices—maybe even leading some to take fanatical action!

What is Reality?

In exploring the truth we would like our evidence to be real. So it's worth thinking about what the term "reality" actually means.

I consider myself to be real. I cannot be a figment of my imagination, because otherwise there would be no "me" to imagine myself. Perhaps everything else is a figment of my imagination, perhaps even my body is a figment of my imagination, but I know (at least that part of me that is able to know knows) that I am real. Descartes captured this in his famous quotation "I think therefore I am."

I am one person. If you were with me there would be two people. And if more and more were to join us we would increase our

---

[8] http://www.jihadwatch.org/2011/11/uk-muslim-students-including-trainee-doctors-walking-out-on-lectures-on-evolution.html accessed 25/2/13

number to 3, 4, 5, and so on. So what are 1, 2, 3, 4, and 5? Whilst there may be 1, 2, 3, 4, or 5 men in a room, there is never just "1." We can have 1 man or even 0 men, but we can't have "minus 1" men, or "minus 1000" men, yet mathematically that is perfectly possible. So are numbers, or indeed any of mathematics real?

On a five pound note it says "I promise to pay the bearer the sum of five pounds." So money represents a promise. In our bank account it's perhaps quite reasonable to have £-1000 as our balance. We owe 1000 promises to someone else. We use both numbers and money daily, and they are invaluable for helping society work. I want some potatoes for my dinner, so I use numbers to decide how many will fill my stomach, and I use my money (promises) to exchange for your potatoes. And at some time in the future you will probably make use of that promise and ask someone else for a pair of trousers. Now you, I, the potatoes and the pair of trousers are what we would normally consider real, but are money and promises?

In the simple example above, we use mathematics (numbers) to represent a quantity of something real. When we do engineering or science, we define properties of the potato; its mass, its volume, its temperature and so on. Then we use mathematics to quantify the amount of those properties; a 300 gram potato for instance. So are the properties of the potato real? We know that a big potato travelling at a high speed will hurt more than a small potato travelling at low speed, so perhaps it is reasonable to conclude of the properties are indeed real.

Once we have defined these properties and given them "Units" to allow us to quantify them (grams in our example above) we can start to do experiments to see how the properties relate to each other. We might see how a given force acting on a potato of a given size causes its velocity to increase. Then we might carry out the same experiment on a bigger and smaller potato to see how the properties of force, mass, and velocity relate to each other. And we define further properties that help us do our sums more effectively (like "Momentum" . . . the mass multiplied by the velocity). Are those combined properties real, or simply concepts?

We capture the relationships between properties in mathematical formulae, and we do mathematical sums on them to predict what will happen in experiments that we have yet to carry out. We might have done all our experiments on a 300 gram potato. We take our deduced formulae to work out what might happen with a 600 gram potato, and then we carry out the same experiments on a 600 gram potato to see if our predictions are right. And we find that the experiment will not quite tie up with our prediction, and so we think a bit more about the formula and whether we have left anything out of our experiment, and we come up with more complex and advanced formulae to predict what the real potato will do in all circumstances. That is what we call science.

So are those complex formulae real? Is an inaccurate formula not real but the more accurate formula real? If all the formulae are wrong, are none of them real? How can something wrong be real? If all of this is what science is, can science be real?

Is Science Real?

Richard Feynman *(US educator & physicist (1918 – 1988))* quoted in a lecture that

> *A philosopher once said that, "It is necessary for the very existence of science that the same conditions always produce the same result."*[9]

It is ingrained in us that each time we carry out the same experiment on the potato we get the same result, but what if we don't? What if the potato doesn't always behave in the same way? It may seem silly to suggest that the potato will not always behave in the same way; our faith in this happening is so deep we are not aware

---

[9] Richard Feynman: "Lecture - The Character of Physical Law Part 6 Probability and Uncertainty" ISBN 978-0140175059 See broadcast lecture on youtube: http://www.youtube.com/watch?feature=player_embedded&v=aAgcqgDc-YM approximately 52 minutes into the lecture

of it. Exactly that faith will be challenged when we come to look at quantum physics later in the book.

But let's get back to mathematics and our friendly potato again. Imagine a light shining on a potato, which is now bouncing up and down on a spring (a bungee potato). The shadow of the potato moves up and down on the wall with a changing speed but in a repeating pattern. Do the same thing with a potato on the spoke of a wheel that is rotating around a spindle and we find that the movement of the shadows of both are the same. We can use the same mathematical formula to describe how the shadow of each moves, but the real objects are moving differently.

Many different forms of equations and mathematical models can be used to describe the same motion. One form uses a concept of an "imaginary" number "i," the square root of minus 1. The name suggests that the number "i" is not real, yet in our formulae it can be used to represent something that is real.

In conclusion, the simple question of what is real is not such a simple question after all. In our day-to-day lives we rely on our common sense and happily decide that some things are real and others are not ("I don't think ghosts are real," for instance). Yet if we scratch below the surface, much of what we dismiss as unreal may not be so.

Atheists and those who believe in God disagree about whether God is real. Before exploring which group might be right we need to be open to what God being real might mean. The question is not as simple as we might think.

Scientific and mathematical equations may or may not be real in the sense of what our common sense tells us, but they are sufficiently real to have a massive effect on our lives. God may not be the same sort of real that we would apply to a potato, but he is very real to those who have found that he has a massive effect on their lives.

What is Faith?

The practical objective of science is to understand the material world and to develop technology for the benefit of mankind. The practical objective of religion is to help us to live a virtuous life, describing or defining the right relationship to God and to each other. Scientific and religious objectives are both morally excellent, and yet underlying both are certain beliefs. We've mentioned the scientific belief that the universe behaves in a repeatable and predictable manner, and of course religion rests on a belief in God. Both science and religion are founded on belief.

But is belief the same as faith? Let's look at some definitions of faith.

Definitions

Anglican priest Michael Green is quoted as saying that "Faith is to commit oneself to act based on sufficient experience to warrant belief, but without absolute proof. To have faith involves an act of will."[10]

Richard Dawkins claims that "Faith is the great cop-out, the great excuse to evade the need to think and evaluate evidence. Faith is belief in spite of, even perhaps because of, the lack of evidence."[11] whereas Mohandas Gandhi commented that "Faith . . . must be enforced by reason . . . when faith becomes blind it dies"[12] and "Unwearied ceaseless effort is the price that must be paid for turning faith into a rich infallible experience."[13]

---

[10] Many internet search results, but I have not found the primary source.

[11]http://www.brainyquote.com/quotes/quotes/r/richarddaw141335.html accessed 25/2/13

[12]http://www.brainyquote.com/quotes/quotes/m/mahatmagan121381.html accessed 25/2/13

[13]http://www.brainyquote.com/quotes/quotes/m/mahatmagan160830.html accessed 25/2/13

Sherwood Eddy claims that "Faith is reason grown courageous"[14]

Although there appear to be conflicting views about faith and thinking, with a little clarification these can be resolved. Clearly Ghandi and Dawkins are in agreement if one clarifies that Dawkins is referring to "blind faith." Eddy would then agree, and add that a reasoned belief needs something more to be turned into faith — courage. To which Green would add "act of will."

All would appear to agree that blind, unthinking faith is bad.

Belief and Faith

There is a difference between belief and faith, and that is action. In the 19th century there was a famous tightrope walker named Charles Blondin. In 1859 he became the first man to cross the Niagara Falls gorge on a tightrope. He added a number of stunts to this achievement including pushing a wheelbarrow across the deep gorge.

The story goes that many people saw Blondin walk across the gorge and believed (on the basis of the evidence of their own eyes) that he was capable of pushing the barrow safely across. However, when he asked whether anyone was willing to be pushed across in the barrow nobody stepped forward. They had the belief, but not the faith. They had seen him do it many times, but were unwilling take the risk that he might not do it another time. They did not trust his abilities sufficiently, so faith requires belief, trust and courage to risk taking an action.[15]

---

[14]http://www.brainyquote.com/quotes/quotes/s/sherwooded10507
2.html accessed 25/2/13

[15] http://www.blondinmemorialtrust.com/witness.html accessed
25/2/13

Figure 1. Stereoscopic picture of Blondin crossing Niagara (Robert N. Dennis collection)

We need faith to reap the benefits of science. We do an experiment, and when we've done it lots of times and the result matches our predictive formula we believe the result. When we start to trust our lives to that result then we have faith. Some people still don't have enough faith to get in an aeroplane. Faith bridges the gap between belief and action. And belief is what one obtains from experience and evidence.

Atheists may consider that their experience leads them to believe that there is no God. However, like all of us their experience is incomplete and their evidence is incomplete and so to be an atheist requires faith. Sometimes atheists are willing to admit this, for example George Klein, an immunologist, commented that "I am not an agnostic. I am an atheist. My attitude is not based on science, but rather on faith . . . . The absence of a creator, the non-existence of God is my childhood faith, my adult belief, unshakable and holy."[16]

Faith in Science

Science is supposed to be objective rather than an act of faith. Yet the following example shows that faith is at the heart of science. NASA describes Dark Matter as the

---

[16] George Klein: *The Atheist in the Holy City*, Cambridge, MA, MIT Press 1990 ISBN 978-0262610773

*. . . name given to the amount of mass whose existence is deduced from the analysis of galaxy rotation curves but which until now, **has escaped all detection**. There are many theories on what Dark Matter could be. Not one, at the moment is convincing enough and the question is still a mystery.*[17]

So why do scientists think Dark Matter exists? By measuring the radiation from distant clusters of galaxies scientists can deduce a corresponding mass of the galaxies. Unfortunately the mass that they calculate does not tie up with the mass that can be observed. In order for the present equations to be correct, some 95% of the universe needs to be Dark Matter and Dark Energy. Many scientists have faith that the present equations are correct, and need something, which they call Dark Matter, to balance the sums. However, other scientists may have less faith in the present equations and are trying to find new ones that better match what is measured.

Faith in Our Opinions

I have found in my investigations that there are at least two interpretations of almost any claimed fact. Different people draw different conclusions from the same piece of evidence. As an example consider free will. Free will is inconsistent with the laws of physics as we know them, and so some people claim that free will is an illusion. From the same evidence, others claim that the existence of free will shows that there is more than just the material universe. The conclusion depends on our set of beliefs, our faith.

Bertrand Russel was an influential atheist in the first half of the last century. In 1927 he presented a talk entitled "Why I Am Not a Christian." to the National Secular Society[18]. I've read a transcript.

---

[17] http://imagine.gsfc.nasa.gov/docs/dict_ad.html#dark_matter accessed 23/2/13

[18] Lecture on March 6, 1927 to the National Secular Society, South London Branch, at Battersea Town Hall. Published in pamphlet form in

It seems that he found none of the arguments put forward as proof of God were overwhelming, and that he found his personal interpretation of the teaching of Christ unattractive. In other words, he didn't want to be a Christian and would not be convinced otherwise.

If an individual really doesn't want to believe in God then it will not be possible to summon arguments to persuade them otherwise. Similarly, it is not possible to persuade someone to atheism unless they no longer want to believe in God. It becomes a decision of the heart whether to believe in God or not.

That is why Russell in 1927 and others since, on both sides of the religious fence, have made good use of emotional devices to defend their position. Russell stated that "Historically, it is quite doubtful whether Christ ever existed at all," a qualitative statement that manipulates the listener—nobody wants to be persuaded to something that is doubtful. Mind controller Derren Brown begins his book *Tricks of the Mind* with "The Bible is not History. Coming to terms with this fact . . ."[19] Yet I have found that there is substantial evidence that Jesus did indeed exist, as I will show later in this book, so what both gentlemen claim as facts are at best misleading.

Russel and Brown are clearly very intelligent atheists, and there are equally intelligent Christians, Moslems, and agnostics. It is clear that there cannot be an irrefutable case either for or against God or any particular religion. Therefore all of these different beliefs must be underpinned by faith.

So in conclusion, each of us must <u>choose</u> what to believe, and we can only do that based on limited data, on personal experience, on reason and on feelings. And for each of us, that is an act of faith, whether we are conscious of it or not.

---

that same year – readily accessible on the internet, e.g.
http://www.users.drew.edu/~jlenz/whynot.html accessed 25/2/13
    [19] *Tricks of the Mind* Derren Brown ISBN 978-1-905-02635-7

Chapter 2: Science Describes an Incredible Universe

Familiarity has been rightly accused of breeding contempt. When pocket calculators first came out, people were excited that you could do a sum which computed to give 71077345, and when you turned your calculator upside down it spelt out SHELLOIL. Compare that with our contempt at a mobile phone that doesn't find all the restaurants in our locality within 10 seconds. We dismiss the enormous amount of development that has brought about this technological advance and take it for granted that the latest model will be out of date within six months.

Similarly, we can become so familiar with the images and explanations on popular science programs that we forget to appreciate how incredible the workings of the universe are. Perhaps part of the difficulty lies in the massive difference in scale between (say) atoms, and what we can see/feel/perceive with our senses. We cannot relate to the descriptions in an accurate way, all that we can manage is to relate to the pictures on popular science TV shows.

In this chapter I will describe many of the findings of science. Much of what science shows us is way beyond our experience of common sense and day-to-day experience. I urge you, as you read these descriptions, to try to grasp the scale of what is described. When I talk about a cell, look at your hand, or a leaf, and imagine how small but complex it is. When I talk about DNA, try to picture it both coiled up and stretched out. When I talk about relativity, try to imagine yourself as a photon emitted at the Big Bang. Science has discovered amazing things about our universe; let's try to get a real appreciation of them.

The Physical Sciences

In this section I will look at the cornerstones of physics: quantum mechanics and relativity, and then see what these theories can tell us about the history and possible future of the universe. I will look at how the history of the universe prepared planet earth for life, at which point the story will be taken up by the biological sciences.

Elemental Particles and Quantum Mechanics.

What is found at the subatomic level is indeed strange, and doesn't conform a bit to our common-sense ideas of how the universe works.[20] This book is not the place to explore the heavy mathematics of quantum theory, but I do want to touch on some of the strange things that we find in the world of subatomic particles. I hope to surprise you at least a little.

Wave and Particle

Light comes in waves. We know that because if we shine a light at a screen with two slits, we see a pattern of dark and light strips on the screen. This is exactly the behaviour we get when waves pass through two slits. Imagine a wave in a tank of water approaching a wall with a slit in it, the height of the water at the slit goes up and down as the wave reaches the slit. The water downstream of the slit only sees the up and down motion at the slit, and this up and down motion causes waves to radiate downstream of the slit. Put two slits close to each other and you have two sets of waves, one radiating from each slit. When the high point of a wave from one slit meets a high point of a wave from the other slit, you get an extra high water level. Similarly, when low points from each slit meet you get an extra low water level. When the high point of one meets a low point of the other, the two cancel out and the water level is zero. If you measure the pattern that the waves make downstream of the slits you will see regions where the waves go up and down

---

[20] *Quantum Theory - A Very Short Introduction* by John Polkinghorne, Oxford University Press, ISBN 0-190280252-6

(where high meets high, and low meets low) and regions where the water level is always the same (where low meets high and high meets low).

We see a static interference pattern created by the waves in the water tank passing through the two slits. We see the same pattern when light passes through two slits onto a screen. Where the waves reinforce (peak + peak, trough + trough) the screen shows a light band, and where they cancel each other you see a dark band.

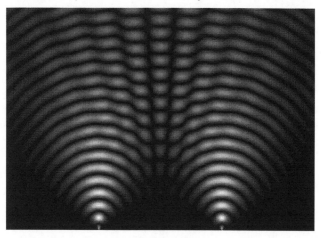

Figure 2. Simulation of the interference of light emerging from two slits

Light comes in particles, called photons. We know that because of what is called the photoelectric effect. When light shines on a metal, the light can knock electrons free from the metal. It takes a certain amount of energy to knock an electron free from the metal. If the light was simply in waves then the amount of energy in the light would be proportional to the amount of light. One would expect that the number of electrons ejected would be proportional to the total energy of light. However, we find that at some frequencies of light there are no electrons ejected, no matter how much light is shone, whereas at other frequencies of light a very dim light will eject some electrons. The ejection of electrons depends on the frequency and quantity of the light rather than just the brightness. This is resolved if the light is considered as a stream of particles of different energy, only a particle of sufficient energy can dislodge an electron, but if the particle doesn't have enough energy then it doesn't matter how many particles you fire at the metal no electrons will be dislodged.

So light comes in both waves and particles. But that brings problems because our common sense tells us that waves and particles behave differently. Look at the two slit experiment: If we were to fire a single particle at a wall containing two slits, it would either bounce back off the wall, go through one slit, or go through the other. If it went through a slit we'd expect to see a mark on the wall behind the slit. What would we expect to happen if we send a stream of particles at a wall containing two slits? We'd expect some to bounce back off the wall, some to go through one slit and some to go through the other, and we'd expect to see two dots on the wall behind the slit. But we know that when we send a stream of photons at two slits we get the interference pattern, so how can they be particles?

And what happens when we send a single photon of light at the two slits? If it is a particle then we would expect it to make a mark behind the slit it passed through. Instead, we find that it might leave a mark anywhere—we simply cannot predict where it will hit the screen.

Send another photon at the slits and it will make a mark somewhere different and again, we have no idea where. But as more photons are fired at the slits, one at a time, we gradually see the interference pattern build up on the screen. But we are firing the photons one at a time, they cannot interfere with each other because only one is passing through the slit at any given time; there is not a second photon to interfere with. Is each photon interfering with itself? How can a single particle interfere with itself? It doesn't form an interference pattern, it can only make a single dot on the screen; but as we said, the position of the dot is unpredictable.

It is possible to measure which slits the photons go through, to see if they all go through both slits? If we do such an experiment, half the photons go through one slit and half go through the other slit. Just what one would have expected from particles. But the strange thing is, when we do this experiment you only see a pattern of two dots on the wall! The interference pattern has disappeared. The light has behaved just like particles and not like waves at all!

From experiments such as this we must conclude that if you are looking for waves then you will find waves, and if you are looking for particles then you will find particles. The act of measuring causes the photon to become one or the other. The same behaviour is found for electrons and other subatomic particles.

What quantum physics shows us is that *before* we measure a photon, it is *both* wave *and* particle and it could be *anywhere*. There is a probability of what and where it is, but it only actually becomes wave or particle in a particular place when it is measured.

Very complex mathematical equations have been developed to predict what you will measure in different situations, but only on average. The predictions appear to match the experimental evidence remarkably accurately. However, although the equations can predict that sufficient photons will produce an interference pattern, it is not possible to predict what a single photon will do. Each photon that registers on the screen will make just one dot, and it's only when you get enough photons that you see the different dots form into the pattern. The behaviour of the crowd appears to be predictable but the individual is not; shine a single photon at two slits and you have no idea where it will hit the screen.

If you thought the universe was common-sense and predictable, it's time to think again. It was this behaviour that prompted Richard Feynman's quote, now shown in full.

> *A philosopher once said "It is necessary for the very existence of science that the same conditions always produce the same results." Well, they do not. You set up the circumstances, with the same conditions every*

*time, and you cannot predict behind which hole you
will see the electron.*[21]

Quantum Entanglement

Let me mention another strange behaviour of subatomic particles: "Quantum Entanglement."

Imagine we take two objects and bump them together in such a way that they cause each other to spin. The direction of the spin on one object is opposite to the direction on the other; one object spinning one way has determined that the other object is spinning the other way. We don't know which object is spinning which way, and so we decide to measure them. Unfortunately, by the time we decide to measure them they are separate by 1000 miles—perhaps when the bumped together they set off in opposite directions at high speed. Up until this point we have not measured either of them, so we don't know the direction of spin of either of them. So we measure one of them (the one that is not 1000 miles away) and see it is spinning anticlockwise. Immediately, we know that the one that is 1000 miles away is spinning clockwise.

We can do this experiment with subatomic particles. We cause two particles to interact such that each has an equal and opposite "Spin" and then separate them by 1000 miles. This is known as quantum entanglement since the two particles become "Entangled" before being separated. But we know from quantum physics that *neither of them actually has a spin until we measure it.* The act of measuring one particle causes its spin, in the same way that measuring a photon as a wave caused it to become a wave. So we measure the spin on one and it immediately has spin. But because the other particle has the opposite spin we immediately know the spin on the other, 1000 miles away. Measuring the spin on one particle has therefore *caused* the spin on the other.

---

[21] Richard Feynman: "Lecture - The Character of Physical Law Part 6 Probability and Uncertainty" ISBN 978-0140175059

You can replace the 1000 miles with 200 billion miles and the same conclusion results. Something happening to a particle in one place has instantaneously influenced another particle 200 billion miles away. The influence has travelled at infinite velocity.

This seems really weird and we might think it a quirk of faulty logic if experiments had not demonstrated the behaviour. The following is from a Scientific American article:

> *If that strikes you as more than a little counterintuitive, you're in good company. Albert Einstein once disparaged quantum entanglement as "spooky action at a distance." As he and his colleagues wrote in 1935, "No reasonable definition of reality could be expected to permit this." Reasonable or no, entanglement indeed appears to be a part of reality, as numerous experiments have demonstrated.*[22]

Space, Time and Relativity

Einstein's theory of relativity is today's rock of astrophysics. It is based on two assumptions, that the speed of light in a vacuum is constant relative to an observer, and that the behaviour of a physical system does not depend on the coordinate system used.

The theory shows that space and time are not the clean, linear properties that people experience in their daily lives, but complex properties which are dependent on the observer. Strong gravitational fields can curve the space-time coordinates. The curvature of space due to the gravitational field of the sun explains why there is a slight variation in the behaviour of the planet Mercury compared with Newtonian theory.[23]

---

[22]http://blogs.scientificamerican.com/observations/2012/02/15/quantum-entanglement-experiments-expand-to-include-eight-photons/ accessed 11/3/13

[23] *The Inexplicable Universe: Unsolved Mysteries* Lecture series. Neil deGrasse Tyson. ISBN 159803851-6

**Figure 3: Curvature of space according to the theory of relativity
(Source NASA)**

Relativity theory predicts that time does not pass constantly for observers who are moving relative to one another. This leads to some strange and non-intuitive conclusions when observers start to travel at high speeds.

Since the passage of time depends on the coordinate system, one observer might see two events happen simultaneously, whereas in the coordinate system of another observer they may happen at different times.

Imagine a spaceship leaves the earth and accelerates to high fractions of light speed towards a distant planet. It then returns. A clock on the spaceship will show a much shorter elapsed time than a clock that is left on earth. The faster the spaceship goes the shorter the elapsed time for the observer on the spaceship. If the spaceship were to travel at the speed of light, the trip would take no time at all. This effect has been demonstrated using very accurate atomic clocks.[24] [25]

---

[24] Ives, H.E.; Stilwell, G.R. (1938). "An experimental study of the rate of a moving clock." *J. Opt. Soc. Am* 28 (7): 215–226

[25] Ives, H.E.; Stilwell, G.R. (1941). "An experimental study of the rate of a moving clock. II." *J. Opt. Soc. Am* 31 (5): 369–374

An implication is that a photon of light (which travels at the speed of light) takes *no time* to reach its destination. This means that those photons that are now reaching us from the distant galaxies formed in the Big Bang have, in their own frame of reference taken no time to reach us. They still travel at the speed of light, but for no time to have elapsed they have travelled no distance. As far as the photon is concerned, the physical space that it occupied at the Big Bang is here and now, and the universe is really young!

Quantum entanglement shows that it takes no time for information to travel between two entangled particles. Relativity shows that travel at the speed of light reduces distances to zero so it takes no time for a photon to reach its destination. Physics is not just common sense.

Physical Constants

A fundamental assumption of Einstein's theory of relativity is that the speed of light relative to an observer is constant in a vacuum. The value of the speed of light constant "c" (measured in metres per second for instance) changed over the years as more refined measurements brought in more accurate results, see the chart.[26] [27]

---

[26]http://math.ucr.edu/home/baez/physics/Relativity/SpeedOfLight/measure_c.html accessed 30/3/13

[27] http://www.raman-scattering.eu/raman/texts/009_menu_vitesse.php accessed 30/3/13

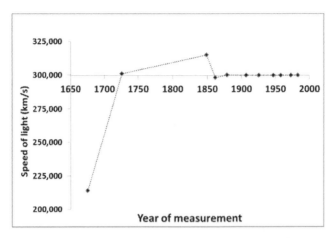

Figure 4. Change in the measured speed of light

It has not changed since 1983, when the 17th Conférence Générale des Poids et Mesures decided that instead of measuring the distance travelled to determine the value of the speed of light, it would be better to fix the speed of light and to redefine the length of one metre to be "the length of the path travelled by light in vacuum during a time interval of 1/299,792,458 of a second."

A change in the measured speed of light does not necessarily mean that the speed of light is not constant; we only know that that our measurement of it changed.

However, there are other constants where a change over time would be significant. Some constants are non-dimensional ratios, like π (pi) the ratio of the circumference to the diameter of a circle. Whilst π can be determined mathematically, some non-dimensional constants have to be measured. One such constant is the fine structure constant alpha (Greek letter α). This is assumed constant, but there are indications that it may not be. Dr Michael Murphy describes the situation:

> *Put briefly, a fundamental constant is a number that is central to a given theory -- that is, to calculate/predict the results of an experiment, you need to know that number. But you can't use known theories to calculate that number -- it must be*

measured in an experiment. In essence, these numbers are fundamental because we have no idea where they come from! And since no one knows how to calculate their values, and because we do find the same value with different experiments conducted at different times/places, we assume that these numbers are, in fact, constants. The experiments we conduct tend to be limited to laboratories on the earth during the last 100 years or so. But what if the constants are/were different in different places in the universe or at different epochs in cosmic history? An experiment should test the constancy of the constants in these extreme cases.

Our experiment picks on one very well-known constant: the fine structure constant, alpha. This constant is the central parameter in electromagnetism -- the theory of how light and matter interact. Alpha is a combination of other constants that you might be more familiar with: alpha = e2/hc where c is the speed of light, e is the charge of an electron and h is Planck's constant. Thus, alpha is important for a relativistic (i.e. c) quantum mechanical (i.e. h) theory of electromagnetism (i.e. e). But alpha is, in some sense, more fundamental than these other constants. Alpha is known to exquisite precision from laboratory measurements:

1/alpha = 137.035 999 074

with an experimental uncertainty of just 0.000 000 044! But was alpha the same, say, billions of years *ago? Or was/is it the same in extremely distant regions of the universe?*[28]

Murphy and others have been making measurements of alpha and have published[29] [30] the results of measurements that appear to show that alpha does indeed vary across the universe. The conclusion is not universally accepted yet, as it may be subject to experimental error, but the belief that alpha should be constant is based on a very few measurements compared with the scale of the universe and should be recognised as an assumption at present.

How Old is the Universe and What is in It?

If we watch a firework explode, we can see that it starts from a point and all the sparks radiate out from that point. If we were to take a snapshot measurement of the direction and speed of each spark we can use the equations of motion to work out where they came from, and so deduce where the firework first exploded. However, we need both our measurements of the sparks and the equations of motion to be correct in order to get the right answer

Consider the universe today as the snapshot measurement. We can run Einstein's theory of relativity in reverse to determine what the universe might have been in the past. The result will depend on the accuracy of our measurements today and on the detailed equations, so we cannot be completely sure what happened, but we can get some good insights.

---

[28] http://www.astronomy.swin.edu.au/~mmurphy/res.html accessed 30/3/13

[29] http://arxiv.org/abs/1202.4758v1 Spatial variation in the fine-structure constant -- new results from VLT/UVES: Julian A. King, John K. Webb, Michael T. Murphy, Victor V. Flambaum, Robert F. Carswell, Matthew B. Bainbridge, Michael R. Wilczynska, F. Elliot Koch

[30] http://arxiv.org/abs/1008.3907 Indications of a spatial variation of the fine structure constant: J. K. Webb, J. A. King, M. T. Murphy, V. V. Flambaum, R. F. Carswell, M. B. Bainbridge

Cosmic Egg

The idea of a universe that expanded from a single point was first suggested by physicist, astronomer and priest Georges Lemaitre in 1931.

> *He proposed that the universe expanded from an initial point, which he called the 'Primeval Atom' and developed in a report published in Nature. Lemaître himself also described his theory as 'the Cosmic Egg exploding at the moment of the creation;' it became better known as the 'Big Bang theory,' a pejorative term coined by Fred Hoyle who was a proponent of the static universe.*
>
> *This proposal met scepticism from his fellow scientists at the time. Eddington found Lemaître's notion unpleasant. Einstein found it suspect because he deemed it unjustifiable from a physical point of view.*[31]

Today we are aware that the "Primeval Atom" is too big an entity to have started with, we know that an atom is not the smallest thing there is. There are many different elemental particles and antiparticles that are much smaller than the atom.

It is impossible to imagine the rending of "Nothing" into matter and antimatter, injecting and releasing vast amount of energy to tear nothingness into something. In the very earliest fractions of the first second after the Big Bang energy levels were so enormous and space was so small that all sorts of particles and antiparticles were being created and destroyed. Applying common sense we can understand that "Nothing = Matter + Antimatter" yet we find that after this creative event the universe is full of matter. This is bizarre; although nothing becomes particle and antiparticle, it seems that if you recombine them then there remains a remnant of particles.

---

[31] http://en.wikipedia.org/wiki/Georges_Lemaitre accessed 25/2/13

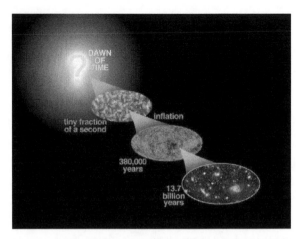

Figure 5. History of the universe (Credit: NASA / WMAP Science Team)

The principle of an initial Big Bang is now almost universally accepted. It was not always so and indeed Einstein at first introduced a "Cosmological Constant" into his theory of relativity in order to make it predict a universe that was not expanding from a single point but was static in size; a static universe. Einstein regarded introduction of the cosmological constant into an otherwise elegant theory as his "greatest mistake," since it was introduced to produce a prejudged outcome. Indeed, measurements do not suggest a static universe, or even one expanding at a constant rate but an accelerating universe.

Dark Matter and Dark Energy

Scientists are gathering a lot of data from the NASA Wilkinson Microwave Anisotropy Probe (WMAP) and the European Space Agency Planck mission, and seeing how well theory matches the data. The predictions do not fit the observations.

In order to make the equations match the measured results, something like Einstein's cosmological constant seems to be needed. Physicists have postulated that there is unobserved "Dark Matter" and "Dark Energy" in the universe and calculated the amount needed to match the measured results.

The amount necessary to tune the equations to observation is quite surprising. The following chart shows the result.

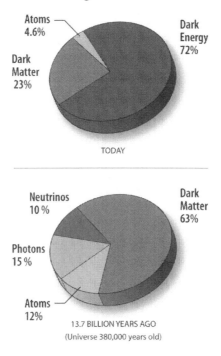

Figure 6. Composition of the universe and change with time
(Credit: NASA / WMAP Science Team)

Intriguingly only 5% of the mass and energy in the model is that which we can observe today. The implication is that 95% of the universe cannot be detected. As NASA puts it:

> *Until about thirty years ago, astronomers thought that the universe was composed almost entirely of this "baryonic matter," ordinary atoms. However, in the past few decades, there has been ever more evidence accumulating that suggests there is something in the universe that we cannot see, perhaps some new form of matter.*[32]

---

[32] http://map.gsfc.nasa.gov/universe/uni_matter.html accessed 30/3/1

NASA has run the relativity equations with different assumptions of the amount of Dark Matter and Dark Energy; this is the result:

EXPANSION OF THE UNIVERSE

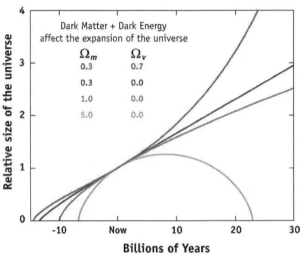

Figure 7. Effect of different proportions of Dark Matter and Energy on the expansion of the universe

Current measurements suggest that the universe is following the red curve, and expanding at an increasingly fast rate. The calculation to match the WMAP data gave an estimate that the age of the universe is 13.7 ± 0.13 billion years. However, recently this estimate has been updated using results from the Planck mission.

> *At a March 21 NASA telephone news conference, scientists from the U.S. team participating in the European Space Agency's Planck mission to map the cosmic microwave background (CMB) discussed Planck's first cosmological results, including some surprising news. For one thing, the universe is 13.82 billion years old, a hundred million years older than previously thought, because it's expanding more slowly.*

Even more surprising is that the universe contains significantly less Dark Energy and significantly more matter—both dark and ordinary—than indicated by the prior CMB surveyor, NASA's WMAP satellite. According to Planck's results, Dark Energy accounts for only 68.3 percent of the mass-energy of the universe, down from WMAP's 71.4 percent, whilst Dark Matter is up 26.8 percent from WMAP's 24. And whilst the ordinary stuff you and I are made of and can see or touch is still a small part of the whole, at least we've climbed back up to 4.9 percent (pretty close to one-twentieth, eh?) from the miserable 4.6 percent we could claim until recently.[33]

Dating Galaxies

In parallel with refining estimates of the age of the universe from relativity, it can also be estimated by determining the age of stars in distant galaxies, although much less accurately.[34] Large stars burn up much faster than small stars, and so from the mass of the largest stars in distant clusters of stars it is possible to infer the age of the cluster. The older the cluster the smaller the largest star will be. In this way, the inferred age of the universe is between 11 and 18 billion years old.

How were the Chemical Elements Made?

Making Helium

Immediately after the Big Bang the first and only available element was hydrogen, the smallest and simplest of all the elements. The carbon and oxygen atoms that comprise just over 80% of our body did not exist; they still needed to be manufactured. The first step towards carbon and oxygen was the manufacture of helium

---

[33] http://newscenter.lbl.gov/science-shorts/2013/03/21/planck-results/ accessed 30/3/13

[34] http://map.gsfc.nasa.gov/universe/uni_age.html accessed 30/3/13

atoms, known as alpha particles (two protons and two neutrons) in an atomic fusion process. This process occurs in first generation stars and the release of energy from this process causes such stars to shine.

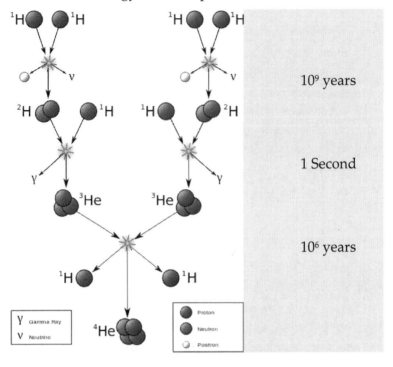

Figure 8. Manufacture of helium in the sun

Two hydrogen atoms combine and give off a positron (positively charged antimatter particle—the opposite of an electron) and a neutrino (an electron with no charge), to form deuterium (the isotope of hydrogen found in heavy water). The average time that a hydrogen nucleus has to wait for the fusion to occur is a billion years, but since there are so many hydrogen atoms in the star there are plenty of reactions occurring at any moment. Shortly after that fusion another hydrogen atom combines to form helium-3 and a gamma ray. Finally a million years later two helium-3 atoms combine to form helium-4 with the emission of two hydrogen atoms.

Each of these steps gives off energy. The deuterium atom has less mass than the two hydrogen atoms that combine to form it. Similarly the helium-3 atoms have less mass than the constituent parts, and so on. The difference in mass is converted to energy in the fusion process, according to $E=Mc^2$. The released energy heats up the star and causes it to shine. Typically these reactions occur at around 10 million degrees centigrade. Over time as the hydrogen gets converted to helium, the reaction rate reduces and the star starts to dim. However, by then there are plenty of helium atoms ready for the next steps of conversion to carbon and onwards to oxygen.

Triple-Alpha Process

The manufacture of carbon from the helium atoms is a two-step process. First, two helium atoms combine to form beryllium-8 then a further helium atom needs to fuse with the beryllium-8 to form carbon. This process is known as the "Triple-alpha process" since the nucleus of the helium atom is an alpha particle and carbon comprises three alpha particles.

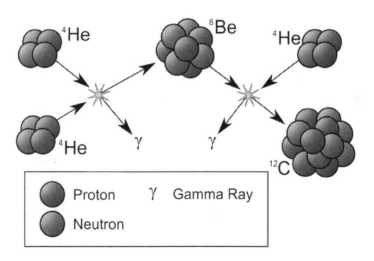

Figure 9. Carbon manufacture by the Triple-Alpha Process

The manufacture process is difficult because beryllium-8 is extremely unstable and will decay back to two helium atoms incredibly quickly, typically 10^{-16} seconds (a tenth of a millionth of a billionth of a second). There is a stable version of beryllium (beryllium-9) that has four protons and five neutrons but that is formed by an entirely different process. In order to produce carbon, the rate at which a third alpha particle fuses with the beryllium-8 needs to be as high as the rate at which the beryllium-8 decays. The rate of fusion of the third alpha particle becomes sufficient only at extremely high temperature, around 100 million degrees centigrade.

Nuclear Resonance

Even at such high temperatures, the chance of the Triple-Alpha process working would normally be very small, and would be insufficient to produce the quantities of carbon that are found in the universe. However, each step is made possible by what is called a "Nuclear Resonance." At extremely high temperatures the beryllium-8 + helium atom reach a resonant state when they are no longer "two alpha particles in one place and one in another" but are in a sort of "togetherness" of three alpha particles. After a short period they decay again, but because of the proximity of the energy levels of (beryllium-8 + helium) and of an excited state of carbon, sometimes (about four in every thousand) they decay into carbon atoms and sometimes (nine hundred and ninety-six times in every thousand) they decay back into beryllium-8 + helium, and then the beryllium-8 decays back to two helium atoms.

Fred Hoyle predicted that such a resonance must exist, even though it had not been found at the time, in order to explain the abundance of carbon in the universe.[35] One of his colleagues, William Fowler, then conducted experiments which confirmed the prediction. Hoyle further proposed a theory of "Stellar Nucleosynthesis" which describes that all of the nuclei of elements other than hydrogen have been formed in the nuclear reactions taking place in stars, and that hydrogen is the single ancestor of all the elements.

---

[35] Hoyle, F., Dunbar, D. N. F., Wenzel, W. A. and Whaling, W. 1953, *Phys. Rev.* 92, 1095

Fowler was awarded the Nobel Prize "for his theoretical and experimental studies of the nuclear reactions of importance in the formation of the chemical elements of the universe" whereas Hoyle was omitted. Hoyle made a significant contribution to physics, although he was not always in agreement with the established view.[36]

But how can a star reach the 100 million degrees centigrade necessary for the Triple-Alpha process when the hydrogen to helium fusion process only reaches 10 million degrees? When the hydrogen in the core is used up a star moves into the red giant phase. Without the heat generated by the hydrogen fusion reaction, the core starts to collapse under gravity. As the mass concentrates, the release of gravitational energy heats up the core once again, this time to the much higher temperatures needed for the Triple-Alpha process.

Since the Triple-Alpha process releases energy the core may grow again and become unstable, releasing matter into space, or it may explode in a supernova. As the core collapses more, further reactions can occur and manufacture the heavier elements. The heaviest elements found are believed to come from thermonuclear reactions that result from supernova explosions.

The earth is made of elements that are only manufactured in dying stars, and so it was necessary for the processes described above to occur before a planet such as ours could exist. Our sun and solar system would have formed after the debris of earlier stars gathered as a molecular cloud which gradually collapsed under the force of gravity to form our sun and planets. Our sun is what is called a "Population 1" star, with a high amount of "metal" (any elements that are not hydrogen or helium) content. It is some of this metal from the molecular cloud that collapsed to form the earth.

---

[36] http://www.physicsoftheuniverse.com/scientists_hoyle.html accessed 30/3/13

Manufacture of Prebiotic Materials (Amino Acids Etc.).

Soon we will move into the realm of biological science but before we do, there is a little more that the physical sciences need to do to set the stage for the initiation and development of life on earth. The building blocks of life are not just the elements (carbon, oxygen, nitrogen etc.) but more complex molecules. Let's have a look at how some of these prebiotic materials might have been manufactured, and at the chemistry of the early earth.

Since the earth formed from the gravitational collapse of a molecular cloud it would initially have been a molten mass. The crust would have solidified as heat radiated into space, and gravity would draw the heavy elements to the core. The lighter elements would have formed a gaseous atmosphere around the earth, held in place by the gravitational pull of the core.

The early atmosphere would be nothing like our atmosphere today. There would have been little free oxygen, no ozone, maybe water. There may have been simple organic molecules in the atmosphere; carbon monoxide, methane, and ammonia. We find such organic compounds in meteors, in the atmosphere of other planets in the solar system, Jupiter and Saturn, and in interstellar dust clouds, so it is reasonable to conclude that there were such compounds around the earth. The formation of such simple molecules does not pose significant challenges to our experience of chemistry, but prebiotic materials begin to get a little more complex, for example the amino acid glycine comprises nitrogen, carbon, oxygen and hydrogen.

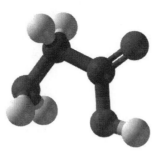

Figure 10. Model of glycine (chemical formula NH₂CH₂COOH)

Miller-Urey Experiment

Back in the 1950s, Stanley Miller and Harold Urey conducted some famous experiments where they filled a vessel with water, methane, ammonia and hydrogen, heated it and discharged electricity to simulate lightning in the flask. After two days they found the amino acid glycine, and a week later they found many other organic compounds that are important raw materials of life, including thirteen of the amino acids used in proteins in living cells.[37]

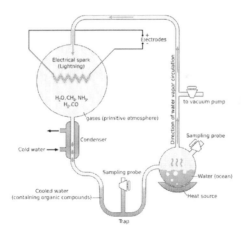

Figure 11. Miller-Urey experiment: manufacture of amino acids

The experiment suggests that given the constituent elemental molecules found in living creatures (oxygen, carbon, hydrogen,

---

[37] "A Production of Amino Acids Under Possible Primitive Earth Conditions" – Stanley L. Miller. *Science*, 1953

nitrogen), the behaviour of the electromagnetic force, and the quantum behaviour of electrons then it is a matter of providing the right conditions to manufacture all of the smaller "Prebiotic" compounds. We can't really describe how they do it in the level of detail that we can model the behaviour of fundamental particles, but the experiment demonstrates that if you put the right ingredients together and provide appropriate input of energy then the manufacture then these more complex molecules will result. We usually assume that this is a result of the interaction of the particle behaviour that we explored earlier in this chapter, but we don't actually know that there is not some further overall system behaviour that drives the process.

We will never know exactly what the conditions were on the early earth but nevertheless, it seems reasonable to suppose that no miraculous event was needed in the formation of the small molecules that are pre-requisites for the life; it is just the way the universe seems to work.

Timeline

Here is a summary of the history of the earth, from the viewpoint of physics.

13.8 billion years ago: universe created

13.5 billion years ago: first stars form

13 billion years ago: larger stars start to explode, generating heavier elements. Smaller stars have longer lifecycles.

5 billion years ago: the Sun forms, perhaps as a second or third generation star.

4.5 billion years ago: The earth formed as a molten mass. For the next 700 million years it was probably bombarded by large objects, and the energy of the collisions probably kept the earth molten up until . . .

3.8 billion years ago: earth crust solidified. Manufacture of prebiotic chemicals needed for the life to exist.

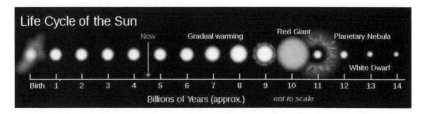

Figure 12. Life cycle of the sun

When the sun reaches the red giant phase, it will have completely consumed the earth if we were to remain in the present orbit, so we might add:

5 billion years in the future: earth consumed when the sun becomes a Red Giant.

In Conclusion

We have moved from the basic theories of physics (quantum theory and relativity) to examine what they tell us about how the universe came into existence, and how it has developed since the Big Bang. We have seen the steps that lead to the production of the elements, and to prebiotic chemicals.

As we move to examine the biological sciences, let's remember that the chemical compounds that are an integral part of life contain subatomic particles with weird wave/particle behaviour and capability to entangle, and the earth sits in a universe where time and space simply don't behave in common-sense ways.

The physical sciences may have developed models to predict the behaviour of large quantities of matter with very good accuracy, but these predictions are based on observation of only a tiny proportion of matter in the universe. Indeed, the present equations require that there is twenty times more matter in the universe than we can detect. And finally, the physical sciences have told us nothing about why the universe is here, like it is.

The Biological Sciences

The physical sciences have given us the raw materials of life. If we now ask how complex life came to be here today, most people will say "evolution." But does everyone have the same understanding of what evolution is?

Evolution

Let's look at some definitions:

> *"Evolution consists of changes in the heritable traits of a population of organisms as successive generations replace one another. It is populations of organisms that evolve, not individual organisms." National Academy of Sciences*[38]

> *"The process by which different kinds of living organism are believed to have developed from earlier forms during the history of the earth." Oxford Dictionary*[39]

> *"The gradual development of plants, animals, etc. over many years as they adapt to changes in their environment" Oxford Advanced Learner's Dictionary*[40]

Considering the National Academy of Sciences definition in a little more detail, evolution is defined as a change across successive generations. It is not for example the change that occurs through the life of an individual organism, such as the growth from child to adult. It is a change in heritable traits, which means that it is a change that the son has compared to the father, but that the son must then pass on to the grandson. The son and grandson are therefore different

---

[38] http://www.nas.edu/evolution/Definitions.html accessed 30/3/13

[39] http://oxforddictionaries.com/definition/english/evolution accessed 31/3/13

[40] http://oald8.oxfordlearnersdictionaries.com/dictionary/evolution accessed 31/3/13

from the father; they have changed, evolved. The definition says nothing of the means of transmitting the change, just that the change must be inheritable. If a father cuts off his arm, then he has changed. And if he cuts off his son's arm the son too has changed, but we would not expect the grandson to be born with one less arm; such a change is not heritable.

The definition also refers to a change in the characteristics of biological populations. If big parents always have big offspring, and small parents always have small offspring, then environmental changes that favour big offspring will shift the distribution of the population to big people. But a later change in the environment that favours small offspring will shift the distribution of the population to small people. Both of these population shifts are changes, are across successive generations, and are heritable, and so they count as evolution.

The second definition is rather different. Here evolution is a process, indeed it is described as *the* process that is believed to have led to the development of the human being from the earliest ancestral bacteria. This is far more encompassing, explains not just any change, but all the changes, it is the complete process.

The third definition is different again. This definition focuses on the adaption to changes in the environment, with no comment about heredity, or successive generations. According to this definition, the increase in obesity that is being recorded in wealthy countries might be considered evolution, even if it is solely be due to eating food and taking less exercise.

These happened to be the first three definitions that I looked up, but I think this demonstrates the need for caution about the use of the term evolution. When we find people making statements about evolution, we don't really know what they are referring to.

Without thinking too much further it is clear that change happens. If we accept that once there were only the simplest bacteria and now there are humans on earth then there must have been a process (or series of processes) that occurred to make that change, and so an appropriate definition of evolution (change) will allow the majority of people to accept that evolution happens. Of the three definitions above, I favour the first. I feel that including anything about the process or mechanism of evolution in the definition is not particularly helpful and imbues a godlike characteristic to the term.

Q: "How did humans develop from bacteria?"

A: "Evolution did it."

seems to me the scientific equivalent of answering, "God did it." and is not really science.

The Origins of the Theory of Evolution

People generally think that Darwin was the founder of evolution, however this was perhaps not the isolated stroke of genius that it is generally assumed to be.

In 1831, eighteen years before Darwin published *On the Origin of Species*, Patrick Matthews published *On Naval Timber and Arboriculture* which included in an appendix:

> *As nature, in all her modifications of life, has a power of increase far beyond what is needed to supply the place of what falls by Time's decay, those individuals who possess not the requisite strength, swiftness, hardihood, or cunning, fall prematurely without reproducing -- either a prey to their natural devourers, or sinking under disease, generally induced by want of nourishment, their place being occupied by the more perfect of their own kind, who are pressing on the means of subsistence.*

And:

> *There is more beauty and unity of design in this continual balancing of life to circumstance, and greater conformity to those dispositions of nature which are manifest to us, than in total destruction and new creation. It is improbable that much of this*

diversification is owing to commixture of species nearly allied, all change by this appears very limited, and confined within the bounds of what is called species; the progeny of the same parents, under great differences of circumstance, might, in several generations, even become distinct species, incapable of co-reproduction.[41]

Darwin later commented:

In last Saturday Gardeners' Chronicle, a Mr Patrick Matthews publishes long extract from his work on "Naval Timber & Arboriculture" published in 1831, in which he briefly but completely anticipates the theory of Nat. Selection . . . it is, certainly, I think, a complete but not developed anticipation! . . . Anyhow one may be excused in not having discovered the fact in a work on "Naval Timber." [42]

And when Darwin was publishing, he was not the only person to have come up with the concept of natural selection. Alfred Russel Wallace had independently written an essay on the topic, which he sent to Darwin in 1858.[43] In July 1858 Charles Lyall and Joseph Hooker presented both Wallace's essay and others from Darwin to the Linnean Society in London.[44]

However, Darwin's book is clearly the authoritative source of what is now considered to be the Theory of Evolution. So having

---

[41] http://www.ucmp.berkeley.edu/history/matthew.html accessed 1/7/13

[42] Charles Darwin. Letter to Charles Lyell, April 10, 1860. https://www.darwinproject.ac.uk/letter/entry-2754 accessed 1/7/13

[43] http://wallacefund.info/biography-wallace accessed 1/7/13

[44] *On the Tendency of Species to form Varieties; and on the Perpetuation of Varieties and Species by Natural Means of Selection.* By CHARLES DARWIN, Esq., F.R.S., F.L.S., & F.G.S., and ALFRED WALLACE, Esq. Communicated by Sir CHARLES LYELL, F.R.S., F.L.S., and J. D. HOOKER, Esq., M.D., V.P.R.S., F.L.S, &c.

quoted some modern definitions, what did Darwin describe evolution to be? Darwin's book *On the Origin of Species* finishes with:

It is interesting to contemplate an entangled bank, clothed with many plants of many kinds, with birds singing on the bushes, with various insects flitting about, and with worms crawling through the damp earth, and to reflect that these elaborately constructed forms, so different from each other, and dependant on each other in so complex a manner, have all been produced by laws acting around us. **These laws, acting in the largest sense, being Growth with Reproduction; Inheritance which is almost implied by reproduction; Variability from the indirect and direct action of the external conditions of life, and from use and disuse; a ratio of increase so high as to lead to a struggle for life, and as a consequence to natural selection, entailing Divergence of Character and the Extinction of less improved forms.** *Thus, from the war of nature, from famine and death, the most exalted object which we are capable of conceiving, namely, the production of higher animals, directly follows. There is grandeur in this view of life, with its several powers, having been originally breathed into a few forms or into one; and that, whilst this planet has gone cycling on according to the fixed law of gravity, from so simple a beginning endless forms most beautiful and most wonderful have been, and are being, evolved.*[45]

---

[45] *On the Origin of Species By Means of Natural Selection, or, the Preservation of Favoured Races in the Struggle for Life* by Charles Darwin, 1859

Figure 13. Charles Darwin around the time that *On the Origin of Species* was published

Darwin describes a mechanism for improving and changing a pre-existing population of organisms which have pre-existing mechanisms for reproduction and transmission of characteristics from one generation to another. The organisms must reproduce abundantly and with variety. Since there are not enough resources to go round the fight for those resources means that only the strongest win and reproduce. Therefore the characteristics that make them strong survive and are transmitted to the next generation. This is a profoundly plausible process for evolution. We can see elements at work today, and our common sense tells us that it will work. However, perhaps we need to be cautious before we agree that it is the *only* mechanism for evolution. Science has a habit of requiring dramatic changes to our theories when we get too attached to them, and there were certainly other evolutionary mechanisms being considered in Darwin's time.[46]

Natural Selection

Cleary we are far more complex entities than the first bacteria that inhabited the world, so how does natural selection actually work to build complexity?

It is easy to see how some simple attributes can be selected through natural selection. Take for example of a herd of gazelles in a cheetah-infested neighbourhood. Those gazelles that run fastest are going to live longer and produce more offspring than those who are slower. So if the attribute of running fast is something that can be passed on from generation to generation then future generations will contain more fast-running offspring. If we assume that the gazelle's genes, its DNA sequences, define that a gazelle will be a fast-running gazelle, and since genes are passed on from parent to offspring then fast-running parents will have fast-running offspring. The fast running gene will be successful and the slow running genes will be eliminated.

Clearly natural selection requires a population with a range of different attributes. Natural selection can only select fast-running gazelles because there are fast running and slow running gazelles. In Darwin's terms, we need *Divergence of Character*. Where does Divergence of Character come from?

Variability can come from variability in our genes. DNA mixing is inherent in many animals' reproduction process; the genes from each parent are mixed up when forming the sperm or egg, and so the offspring have a varied mix of the characteristics of each parent. There are also chance mechanisms for introducing variability and mutation: errors in copying DNA when a cell divides, or damage to the DNA by radiation for example.

---

[46] http://evolution.berkeley.edu/evolibrary/article/history_09 accessed 1/7/13

Mutation

But do mutations actually bring benefit? Isn't it likely that mistakes in DNA copying will actually make the offspring less fit than the parent? If mutations are random and damaging, how can they lead to an overall increase in complexity and functionality over the generations? Do big changes always come about through a series of small changes; did a mouse gradually develop wings and become a bat for instance?

To begin to answer this we must remember Darwin's requirement for a *ratio of increase so high as to lead for a struggle for life*. Whilst most of the offspring may indeed be less fit than the parent, only a small proportion of the offspring needs to be more fit in order for the generation to generation attributes to improve. This is simply because the struggle for life causes the less fit to die.

The following diagram illustrates in simple terms how this might work:

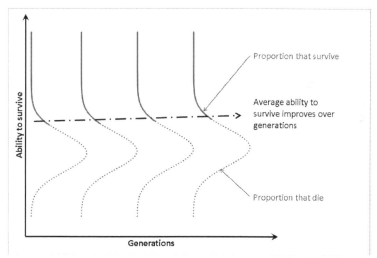

Figure 14. Showing how evolution improves fitness

A parent produces many offspring with varied characteristics. If there are limited resources or there are significant numbers of predators, then only a small proportion of the offspring will survive. Most of the offspring die (or are eaten) and only those who have the necessary attributes to escape death live on to produce the next generation of offspring. The vast majority of the offspring can be less fit than the parent (the peak of the curve shown is lower on the "Ability to survive" scale than the parent). It only needs a very small proportion of the offspring to be better than their parents for the overall ability to survive to improve over the generations.

This is of course a simplified explanation, and it implies that there is a clear single measure of beneficial characteristic. In practice, understanding what a beneficial characteristic is may not be straightforward. To complicate matters, since the environment is always changing, something that is a beneficial characteristic for one generation may not be a beneficial characteristic for subsequent generations. For a robust process, there must still be sufficient variety in the offspring who survive to be ready for significant changes in the environment in the future.

It is also beneficial if there are times of feast as well as famine. When there are sufficient resources it is feasible for the majority of the offspring to survive and for overall population numbers to increase dramatically. This allows diversity to increase, and can allow larger cumulative changes to occur over generations further increasing the complexity of the organism.

Major Transitions

It is clear from the above how characteristics develop through gradual small changes, but it is not immediately obvious that such a process could account for major changes. In their book *The Origins of Life* the authors John Maynard Smith and Eörs Szathmáry identify a number of what they call "Major Transitions" without which we would not exist.[47] The major transitions that they identify are:

1.   From replicating molecules to populations of molecules in compartments

---

[47] *The Origins of Life* – John Maynard Smith and Eörs Szathmáry
ISBN 019 850493 4

2.	From independent replicators to chromosomes

3.	From RNA as gene and enzyme to DNA as gene and protein as enzyme

4.	From bacterial cells (prokaryotes) to cells with nuclei and organelles (eukaryotes)

5.	From asexual clones to sexual populations

6.	From single-celled organisms to animals, plants and fungi

7.	From solitary individuals to colonies with non-reproductive castes (ants, bees, etc.)

8.	From primate societies to Human societies

They state that:

> . . . of the eight transitions that we have listed, we think that all but two were unique, occurring just once in a single lineage. The two exceptions are the origins of multicellular organism, which happened three times, and of colonial animals with sterile castes, which has happened many times. There are interesting implications of the occurrence of six unique transitions, together with the origins of life itself, which we also think to have been a unique sequence of events. Any one of them might not have happened, and if not, we would not be here, nor any organism remotely like us. . .

And later they say that:

> Although we have written of the origin of the eukaryotes as one of the 'major transitions', it was in fact a series of events: the loss of the rigid cell wall, and the acquisition of a new way of feeding on solid particles; the origin of an internal cytoskeleton, and of new methods of cell locomotion; the appearance of a new system of internal cell membranes, including

61

the nuclear membrane; the spatial separation of transcription and translation; the evolution of rod-shaped chromosomes with multiple origins of replication, removing the limitation on genome size; and, finally, the origin of cell organelles, in particular the mitochondrion and, in algae and plants, the plastid.

In other words, their fourth major transition actually includes at least nine more.

Each of these transitions must have given the subsequent organism a survival advantage over the unmodified organism, or at minimum allow co-existence with the original organism. The resulting organism from each transition must have been able to produce copies of itself, either by itself or with a sexual partner; the mutated organism (or pair of organisms) needs to be fertile.

We do seem to have been extremely fortuitous to be here; in Smith and Szathmáry's words:

Any one of them might not have happened, and if not, we would not be here, nor any organism remotely like us.

Evidence for Common Ancestry

We can see from the above that the Theory of Evolution appears sensible and credible, but that there are still some tricky questions. Science is about finding answers to tricky questions, and about finding evidence to test theories. Strong evidence for common ancestry comes from DNA.

When animals reproduce sexually, a random selection of DNA from one parent combines with a similar random selection from the other. The reproduction process ensures that no two fertilised eggs will have the same DNA. Two offspring only have the same DNA when the parent gives birth to identical twins. This occurs when a zygote (the first stage of development from a fertilised egg) splits into two. Each zygote derives from the same fertilised egg and so has identical DNA.

Although DNA differs slightly between people it is recognisably human; nearly all the DNA of one person is the same as nearly all the DNA of another. There is a difference of on average one DNA base in every one thousand between two unrelated people.[48] Because of this it is possible to map the human genome (DNA sequence). The body is very good at ensuring that the sequence of inherited DNA is identical to that in the parent, but occasionally there are copying mistakes and small differences.

Imagine the human DNA to be like a book of the plays of Shakespeare, a long and very precise sequence of letters. When we produce offspring, each parent makes a copy of half of the plays, and the other parent makes a copy of the other half. Each parent makes the copy from the copy that they received from their parents (the grandparents), and endeavours to copy letter by letter without making any errors. Most of the copy will be completely accurate, but occasionally there will be a mistake, introduced at random places. Mistakes with then be transmitted to later copies. There will be the same mistakes in the father's copy that there were in the grandfather's copy of those plays that he got from his grandfather, and the same mistakes as in those plays that he got from the grandmother. So the father's set of mistakes will be unique to himself. The same thing goes for the mother.

Therefore if we look for mistakes in a child's copy we will find the same mistakes in parents' copies and confirm who the child's parents are; and that is basically how DNA testing for parentage works.

Common Ancestry

The Theory of Evolution tells us that humans and other animals have common ancestry, so how does our DNA compare with

---

[48]http://science.education.nih.gov/supplements/nih1/genetic/guide/genetic_variation1.htm accessed 1/4/13

that of other animals and does a comparison support the theory.[49] In particular how does our DNA compare with that of our closest related species, the apes?

Our DNA is coiled into a number of discrete strands called chromosomes. Humans have 23 pairs of chromosomes ranging in length from nearly 47 million to 245 million base pairs. Apes have 24 pairs of chromosomes, of which 22 are extremely similar to human chromosomes. If the last two were joined together then they would match the 23rd human chromosome.

The full chromosome comparison between the chimp and human is shown below:

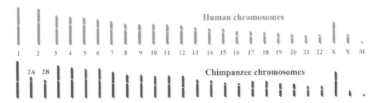

Figure 15. Comparison of human and chimpanzee chromosomes

Using the analogy of the DNA being Shakespeare's plays, both chimp and human have 22 out of 23 of the same plays of Shakespeare. Humans have a 2nd play that has identical words to the combined 2A and 2B plays in a chimp; humans have Henry IV parts 1 and 2 as a single play. With such a close match of the content of the plays, one has to conclude that at some point in the past they both had an ancestor who wrote the original of the plays. The process of copying led to two of the plays being combined into one at some point in the human's past, and no doubt there will have been other changes that accumulated over the generations. However, extremely close similarity of the content of the play is strong evidence for the same original author. DNA evidence such as this makes a compelling case for common ancestry.

---

[49] National Academy of Sciences and Institute of Medicine (2008). *Science, Evolution, and Creationism*. Washington, D.C.: The National Academies Press

Mutant Offspring

However, common ancestry does raise questions. Human chromosome 2 was formed by the linking of two chromosomes of one of our ancestors, an ape of some sort. This change can only have happened in one go: either the chromosome was linked or it wasn't. Did a chance event only happen once or did it occur in two or more offspring at once?

If the linking happened only once (which seems the most likely explanation for a chance event), then the joining of the chromosomes cannot have by itself produced a new species; the single offspring must have been able still to breed. Suppose for instance that the chromosomes linked due to a mistake in the reproduction process, that one change cannot have been sufficient to cause the change in species between apes and humanity, the human would only have been able to breed with another human. It would seem more likely that the joining of the chromosomes was only a small developmental change that left the offspring still able to breed with remainder of the colony.

If the evolved offspring have to be able to breed with the non-evolved offspring, how do we get new species? Whilst one step is not sufficient, if there are separated groups of a given animal then a sufficient number of evolutionary steps taken in each group may lead to the two groups becoming significantly different and unable to interbreed anymore. At that point they can be classed as different species.

When the two chromosomes linked, did the offspring still look like an ape or did it look like a human? Scientists have done many experiments on mutating fruit flies. They find that bombarding fruit flies with radiation causes changes in their DNA. Sometimes this results in changes in the shape of the fruit fly. A single modification of the DNA can lead to significant morphological changes such as extra wings, or different sized and shaped wings. Small changes in DNA do not always cause small and gradual changes in the resultant animal, so perhaps the linking of the chromosomes also led to the ape looking human.

There are, unsurprisingly, many unanswered questions about the evolutionary process. However, there is little doubt that Darwinian evolution happened and continues today.

What Makes Up a Human?

The body itself is an immensely complex and refined organism. It is more complex than the most advanced machine that human beings have ever designed.

Contained within the skin are muscles, organs, a nervous system, a circulatory system, an immune system, a digestive system, a reproductive system, a repair system, a growth system, and perhaps the most complex of all, a brain.

Components

We have nearly 2 square metres of skin, covered mostly with very fine hair, with 100,000 hairs on the head. The soles of our feet are made of hard skin, the underside of our arms is soft. Our skin adapts to how we use it; if we walk barefoot the skin thickens. Our fingerprints are unique. Formed before we are born they remain the same shape throughout our life, even as our hands grow, or become calloused, or as the skin thins as we grow old.

We have around 650 muscles attached to over 200 bones, which vary in size from the femur in our thigh to the stirrup bone in the ear. The muscles can generate the explosion of power needed for a 100m sprint, or the gentlest touch of an artist painting a miniature. The bones in the body are each specifically shaped for their function, articulated with lubricated joints. The muscle/bone system has the precision to throw a dart eight feet into a bull's eye, or to putt a golf ball twenty feet into a hole.

The bones are being continually renewed; all the bone in a child is replaced every year as the child grows. Two types of cells are active in the bone: osteoclasts break down the bone and osteoblasts form new bone. The shape of the bone adapts to minimise the stresses for the load that it carries. The continual destruction and rebuilding of the bone allows a controlled increase in size as a child grows.

Systems

The different parts of the body are supplied with oxygen and nutrients through a complex circulatory system. 60,000 miles of arteries and veins branch repeatedly to reach the most extreme parts of the body. Half of the system circulates de-oxygenated blood through the lungs to be re-oxygenated, and half of the system distributes the oxygenated blood around the body. The pumping heart has four chambers, two for each half of the circulatory system. The first chamber sucks in the blood returning from either the lungs or the body, and then transfers it through a valve to the second chamber which provides the high pressure thrust to send the blood through the lungs or the body. The second chamber is equipped with a valve to prevent backflow. The veins have non-return valves to ensure that blood only flows in the right direction.

Nutrients, food and drink, are taken into the body through the mouth. The tongue identifies that food is good to eat, and guides the food to the 32 teeth that macerate it into small enough parts to pass down the throat to the stomach. The teeth are powered by a strong lever system, the jaw. The sharp front teeth cut and tear the food, the rear teeth being closest to the fulcrum are for grinding. The macerated food is diverted by the epiglottis into the correct pipe into the throat; there is a parallel pipe from the mouth to the lungs. The food is received into a storage and mixing container, the stomach. The stomach walls secrete acids and enzymes that kill bacteria and break down the food into useable chemicals. Muscles around the stomach mix the food and chemicals, and an outlet muscular valve passes the partially digested food through to the small intestines. The stomach digests the food, but does not digest itself.

Six metres of small intestines secrete more enzymes into the food, and begin absorbing the nutrients. The digestion process breaks carbohydrates into simple sugars, fats into fatty acids and protein into amino acids. These small molecules circulate in the blood for use where needed in the body. One and a half metres of large intestine removes the water from the digested waste and discharges it through the anus.

The urinary system filters the blood and clears waste chemicals from the body.

The mouth connects to 2500 kilometres of pipes in the lungs with a surface area of about seventy square metres; the same size as one end of a tennis court. The walls of the lungs are about 1/50th of the thickness of tissue paper and exchange oxygen in one direction and carbon dioxide in the other. A system of mucus and tiny hairs purges the lungs of dust, smoke and debris that are breathed in. The mucus traps the particles and the tiny hairs beat rapidly to push the mucus up the airways to the throat. Hairs in the nose also filter the incoming air, but the mouth can bypass the nose when more flow is needed.

The immune system responds rapidly to attack from bacteria, viruses and chemicals. Within the lymph nodes are billions of B cells, each of which is different and each of which defends against a particular very specific infection.

There is an extravagant reproductive system. At birth a woman's ovaries contain over a million eggs, each of which contains a scrambled subset of her DNA. A man will produce around 400 billion sperm in his lifetime, again with each containing a scrambled subset of his DNA. The complex scrambling mechanism ensures that after mixing of the DNA there is always just the right amount for the new offspring. The act of reproduction in humans is particularly enjoyable and encourages adults to mate and produce offspring.

Brain and Senses

The 1.5kg brain contains around 100 billion neurons, of 10,000 different types. Each neuron has thousands of synapses (input connections from other neurons) and each synapse has perhaps a thousand molecular-scale switches. One human brain is estimated to contain more switches than the entire Internet.[50] [51]

The nervous system transmits signals from the brain throughout the body, controlling every aspect of our daily life. A hair's-width bundle of nerves can contain 100,000 separate wire-like nerve cells. Individual nerve cells can be several feet long.[52]

The endocrine system disperses chemicals into the bloodstream to cause changes in the body. These chemicals, called hormones can instigate longer-term changes, such as preparing the body for pregnancy.

We can hear sounds from 20 to 20,000 Hz frequency, as quiet as pin dropping and as loud as a rocket launch. The 107 million cells in our eyes are able to detect a single photon. The brightest light the eye can detect is a billion times brighter than the dimmest. The eyes adapt their sensitivity first with an iris and then by desensitising the receptor cells.

The body comprises fifty trillion cells which together perform all that is described above and more. All of these cells grew from one single fertilised cell.

Cells, the Building Blocks of the Body

All the components of the body are made up of cells. Whilst the general features of each cell are similar, individual cells are extremely different. The cell is like a little body in itself and comprises a number of miniature organs (called organelles) contained with the cell membrane.

---

[50] http://news.cnet.com/8301-27083_3-20023112-247.html accessed 1/4/13

[51] Single-Synapse Analysis of a Diverse Synapse Population: Proteomic Imaging Methods and Markers – "Neuron" magazine http://www.cell.com/neuron/abstract/S0896-6273(10)00766-X#Summary accessed 1/4/14

[52] http://www.enchantedlearning.com/subjects/anatomy/brain/Neuron.shtml accessed 1/4/13

The cell membrane is made of a lipid bilayer. A lipid is better known as a fat, and is a long hydrocarbon molecule which has a water loving (hydrophilic) head and water hating (hydrophobic) tail. When a small quantity of lipid molecules is dropped into water a lipid would naturally form a droplet with the heads facing the water and the tails keeping as far away from the water as possible. Think of dropping oil into water, it forms a round droplet on the surface. The heads can also be kept facing the water and the tails keeping away from the water if the molecules form a bilayer.

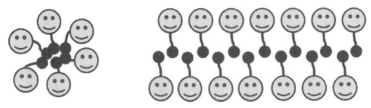

Figure 16. Lipid molecules in a droplet or bilayer

The cell membrane is thus a water impermeable membrane, like a plastic bag that keeps the bits of the cell together. It protects from the outside environment. Embedded in the membrane there are hundreds of proteins that carry out gate-like functions, allowing selective transfer of chemicals across the cell membrane, and others act as sensors, responding to chemicals outside of the cell. Other protein combinations act as machines to propel the cell through a liquid (e.g. the tail on the sperm cell). So the complete cell membrane is a complex interface between the internals of the cell and the outside world.

Organelles

Within the cell are organelles; sub-cell structures which perform specific functions in the operation of the cell.

The nucleus, which is responsible for storing and controlling the DNA for making proteins.

The Ribosome, which translates the DNA into proteins.

The mitochondrion, which is responsible for energy production.

The Vacuole, which is a store for water and fluids.

The Lysosome, which breaks down large molecules into smaller molecules.

The Endoplasmic Reticulum, which transports chemicals around the cell.

The Golgi apparatus, which packs the products from the Endoplasmic Reticulum and the Ribosome to send elsewhere in the cells.

The cytoskeleton, which is the skeleton or scaffolding within the cell. This is also used for transport within the cell and cell reproduction.

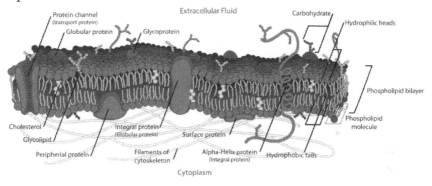

Figure 17. Diagram of cell membrane with embedded proteins

Proteins

Most functions in a plant or animal cell are carried out by proteins: extremely long chains of amino acid molecules. Most potential amino acid chains are either unstable or perform no useful purpose within a cell. Only when amino acid chains perform useful functions in life are they called proteins. Titin protein, found in muscles, is the longest human protein with a length of 34350 amino acids. Amusingly the titin protein in mice is longer, containing 35213 amino acids. The shortest protein chains contain around 150 amino acids. In a protein, the chain is folded into a specific shape and held in that shape by cross linkage bonds along the chain.

There are around 300 known amino acids. Some can be manufactured in laboratories, some have been found in meteors. Only twenty different amino acids are found in living things. Amino acids can bond to each other with different sorts of bond. However, in living organisms they always bond with a left-hand peptide bond. Any one amino acid is able to bond equally easily with any other amino acid. There is nothing in the chemistry that causes one amino acid to bond more frequently with any other.

In order for the protein to perform its function in a cell, it must be the right sequence of amino acids, and it must fold into the right shape. In order for the cell to manufacture a protein, it needs a mechanism that will ensure that each amino is added to the chain at the right time and place, with the right bond. Since there is no chemical reason for one amino to bond with any other it would take approximately $150^{20} = 10^{197}$ tries to assemble even a short protein chain of around 150 amino acids in the right sequence. Cells don't rely on chance; they use a sort of assembly jig to build the protein. It's called DNA.

DNA

DNA (deoxyribonucleic acid) is not a protein; it is not made up of amino acids, but it is a long chain molecule. The components of DNA are nitrogenous bases that are joined together by a backbone of sugar and phosphate molecules. The picture shows two strands of DNA wound together in the familiar double helix shape.

Figure 18. DNA and nitrogenous bases

The stick-like shapes represent the nitrogenous bases and the smooth spiral part of the picture represents the sugar/phosphate backbone. There are only four types of base: Adenine, Cytosine, Guanine and thymine, usually referred to by their initials, A, C, G and T.

Although the backbone is shown as a smooth spiral in the picture, it is a chain of molecules linked together by strong intra-molecular bonds. There are two chains, each forming a spiral helix shape, hence the name "Double Helix." Each backbone carries a chain of bases. Each base on one chain is opposite a unique base on the opposite chain: Adenine is always opposite thymine, and Cytosine is always opposite Guanine. These base combinations are called base pairs.

Although along one chain the bases could be in any order that they choose, once the order on one chain is known then there can only be one order on the other: the order of the complimentary bases from the base pairs.

CGATTCACGATCCG on one strand always matches

GCTAAGTGCTAGGC on the other

These bases between the chains are linked together by weak intermolecular hydrogen bonds. These bonds can be fairly easily broken and reformed, rather like the glue on post-it notes, for reasons that will become apparent later. The bases only bond with the backbone; they do not bond with or interact with each other. This makes it possible for each strand of the molecule to have any sequence of bases. The only reason that the nitrogenous bases stay in a given order is that they are securely bonded by the backbone. It is possible to make any sequence of DNA bases and hold them securely in place with the backbone.

The sequence of bases can act as a code representing to a given sequence of amino acids in a particular protein. Each amino acid is represented by three bases on the DNA code, for instance the DNA sequence "CUA" is the code for Leucine, and "GGU" is the code for glycine. The sequence of bases on the DNA corresponds to the sequence of amino acids in the protein by using a unique three letter code. In this way the DNA is providing the assembly template for the protein molecule.

DNA molecules are incredibly long, containing 3 billion bases in a human. The unravelled DNA of a single cell in a human would be almost 2m long.[53] Only a 3% of the total length of a DNA molecule acts as a template to define the sequence of amino acids in a given protein. For many years the rest of the DNA was considered "junk DNA," although controversial recent research is showing that what was previously written off as junk may be important in helping each cell become the type of cell that it needs to be.[54][55]

DNA itself doesn't produce protein. Proteins are strings of amino acids, and amino acids don't attach to DNA. So an intermediary is needed. That comes in the form of another molecule RNA (ribonucleic acid).

RNA

RNA is similar to DNA, in that it is a long chain molecule made up of a sequence of bases joined together by a backbone. The backbone is similar to DNA, but contains a different sugar. One of the four bases is different too (uracil in RNA instead of thymine in DNA). Unlike DNA, RNA exists as a single strand. It is less stable, and so forms much shorter chains.

Since RNA is only a single strand, the bases are exposed and tend to stick to one another to form complex folded shapes. (Imagine sticky spaghetti in a saucepan forming folded up shapes.) However, any sequence of RNA bases can only stick to a suitable

---

[53] *The Thread of Life* - Susan Aldridge – ISBN 0 521 46542 7 – page 11

[54] http://www.genome.gov/27549810 accessed 1/7/13

[55] http://www.guardian.co.uk/science/2013/feb/24/scientists-attacked-over-junk-dna-claim accessed 1/7/13

complimentary sequence elsewhere on the chain. For instance in the diagram, on the top vertical string, C connects with G, C with G, U with A, and so on; the sequence on one part of the RNA strand GCGGAU will stick nicely to the sequence CGCCUA on another part. Other bond sequences elsewhere create a well-defined three dimensional shape.

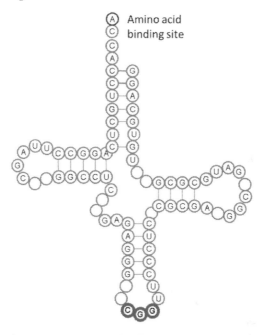

Figure 19. Transcription RNA molecule

In the particular RNA example shown above, the section labelled "Anticodon" has three bases exposed. These three bases can join with three bases on an exposed string of DNA. Additionally, the region labelled "Amino acid binding site" can bond with only one specific amino acid. A specific RNA molecule therefore attaches to a specific amino acid and exposes a specific 3 base sequence of the RNA code. Therefore a specific RNA molecule can act as the intermediary between the DNA code and a specific amino acid. These specific RNA molecules are called "Transcription RNA" (TRNA); each amino acid has its own special TRNA molecule.

In very simple terms (we will look at what actually happens in more detail very soon) we could imagine unzipping the DNA by breaking the weak hydrogen bonds between the two strands (the post-it glue), then attaching an appropriate TRNA molecule to the exposed bases. A number of TRNA molecules could then position their amino acids in the right sequence to form a protein.

How the Cell Works

The sections above describe the components that make up a human being, but not what they do. The following are very simplified (but nevertheless complex) descriptions of how the cells in our bodies work individually and as a whole system.

Signals

There are thousands of proteins embedded in the wall of the cell. One type, called receptor proteins pass messages from the outside of the cell to the inside. These long chain molecules cross the cell membrane, with half of the protein dangling on the outside the cell and half on the inside. The outside part of the protein is the right shape to fit a particular molecule, perhaps a hormone. When the hormone appears outside the cell it attaches to the outer half of the protein. This changes the chemistry and electrical charge distribution of the protein, changing its shape—remember that they are very long complex folded up shapes. This change in the shape affects both the outside and inside halves of the protein.

Because the half of the protein inside the cell changes we can see that a message has been transmitted through the cell membrane that tells the inside of the cell that the hormone is outside the cell. The cell membrane has kept the hormone outside of the cell, but the receptor protein has allowed a message to be transmitted across the cell membrane. Now the message needs to be read and acted on by something on the inside of the cell.

On the inside of the cell is a so-called pathway protein that is the right shape to attach itself to the changed shape of the receptor protein; it could not attach to the original shape. The pathway protein now also changes and attaches itself to an enzyme, causing the enzyme to be active. The enzyme produces a signal molecule which finds its way into the nucleus, where the DNA is stored.

Reading the DNA

The DNA in each human cell is around 1.8m long and yet it fits in a cell that is too small for the naked eye to see. It does this by multiple coiling as shown in the picture. In the first level the DNA is coiled around proteins called histones. The coiled length of the DNA is of the order of 1/100000 meter. The coiled DNA is called a chromosome. With such complex coiling, only some of the DNA is exposed and so it may not be possible to get to the part of the DNA that is needed in response to the hormone outside of the cell. However, there are specific sections on the histone proteins that are the target for our signal molecules. When the signal molecule joins the histone, this causes the required part of the DNA to unravel and become exposed.

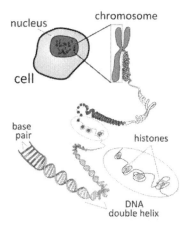

Figure 20. DNA coiling to form a chromosome

A molecule called RNA-polymerase then attaches itself to the exposed portion of DNA. The RNA-polymerase first separates the two strands of DNA, exposing the DNA bases. The RNA-polymerase now manufactures a string of RNA that matches the series of bases on the DNA code, so-called Messenger RNA (MRNA). The bases of the MRNA match the bases on the DNA string so that for example the RNA-polymerase converts a DNA sequence of ATCG into a MRNA sequence UAGC.

At the end of the required section of the DNA string, a special sequence of DNA base pairs tells the RNA-polymerase to stop producing the Messenger RNA. The MRNA is then released and floats off into the cell.

Messenger RNA

Next, the cell's ribosome gathers both the MRNA molecule and the Transcription RNA (TRNA) molecules that we heard about earlier, complete with attached amino acids. The ribosome enables the three exposed bases on a given amino acid/TRNA combination to bond with three corresponding MRNA bases. Then the ribosome enables another amino acid/TRNA combination to join the MRNA, once again with the TRNA bases corresponding to the next three bases on the MRNA string.

When finished, the ribosome has arranged the amino acids in the precisely defined order corresponding to the sequence of original DNA bases that were exposed when the signal molecule attached to the histone tail.

The amino acids are not only in the right sequence, but the shape of the Transcription RNA is such that they are also in the right orientation to form peptide bonds and become a protein chain. As the amino acids join the chain, they part company from their TRNA which then floats off into the cell.

Finally the protein chain molecule is folded into the right shape to perform its job.

Chain of Events

Here are the steps that I've just described: Chemical signal > Attaches to receptor protein outside cell membrane > changes shape of protein > shape inside the cell membrane changes > pathway protein attaches to changed shape receptor protein inside cell membrane > pathway protein attaches to enzyme and activates it > enzyme produces signal molecule > signal molecule goes to nucleus

> signal molecule attaches to histone tail > required part of DNA exposed ready for transcription > polymerase attaches to DNA > polymerase produces RNA string (MRNA) > Ribosome attaches to the end of the MRNA > Ribosome gathers TRNA molecules and assembles amino acid chain > amino acid chain is folded into the right shape and becomes the protein > protein carries out required function in the cell.

This rather general and simplified description is an example of many different tasks being carried out every second of our life in each of the cells throughout our bodies. If any step in the sequence does not occur then the process simply doesn't work. There are some excellent animations of the complex molecular machinery that makes cells work. For example: http://www.dnalc.org/resources/3d/12-transcription-basic.html

It certainly seems that the cell knows what it is doing.

How the Body Works

Different types of cell respond differently to an external stimulus. Each cell is tuned for its particular purpose. So how do all the different sorts of cell work together in order to enable the complete body to function? Let's look at a chain of events that the body orchestrates in response to frightening image.

Stress Response

A man sees a growling Rottweiler a few feet away from him. First the photons of light emitted by the Rottweiler are focused through the lens of the eye onto the retinal cells. These cells transmit their signals through the optic nerve to the brain. The brain recognises the image and the changing behaviour of the image to be that of a snarling dog. That causes the hypothalamus to initiate a stress response. Electrical and chemical signals are now sent around the body. The electrical signals are fastest and may initiate an immediate physical response—causing the person to "freeze" for instance. However chemical signals are secreted into the bloodstream.

The same chemical signal, let's say adrenaline, causes different responses in different cells. The adrenaline will cause the tiny muscles supporting the hairs on our skin to contract making the hairs stand on end, it will cause the muscles around the sweat glands to contract and squeeze sweat onto the skin surface, and it will cause the muscles around the bronchioles in the lung to relax, increasing the lung capacity and allowing more oxygen into the blood. The adrenaline will dock onto cells in the heart, causing it to beat faster and send more blood around the body. Whilst the signal molecule is the same, the protein "machinery" in each muscle cell is different and so the response is different.

The adrenaline signal molecule can cause other cells to release other signal molecules. A cascade of signalling molecules and electrical signals cause the different cells in the body to perform their required function, and combine to produce a magnificently orchestrated body response to the Rottweiler.

Similar actions are happening every moment of every day, when we walk, eat, play with our computers, or drive. Everything we do involves cells working together. Groups of cells are organised into the major functional systems do the day-to-day work of living. Let's look at one of them.

Immune System

Our body also has an immune system to defend itself from attack at a microbial level. This system can recognise and destroy invading cells, but it doesn't attack the body itself. There are many types of infection and the body has many lines of defence, the most powerful of which is an army of a billion "B" cells each primed to destroy an infection. One of the billion different types of B cells is likely to be a perfect match for fighting a particular infection.

The infection will activate that particular B cell, via a receptor protein in the membrane. The B cell will then start to divide and make copies of itself, rapidly increasing the number of "activated" B cells to match the number of infecting agents. Each copy produces and releases antibodies that then attach to the infection and signal it for destruction by other systems in the body.

Each B cell has different receptors and produces different antibodies. The antibodies (which are proteins) are manufactured from the DNA code within the B cell. Therefore the billion B cells all have different DNA.

The B cells are produced within the bone marrow in a process which cuts up and reassembles sections of our DNA in a complex splicing process. One of our chromosomes has a special portion of DNA that is used for this process. The DNA has regions containing short sequences of DNA, so-called "V," "D" and "J" regions. There are perhaps 100 different V portions, 20 different D portions and 6 different J portions. Each B cell has a section of DNA has just one V,D and J portion. A random process selects which portion of V,D and J is in a given cell, and so as more and more B cells grow in our bone marrow the number of variants will increase until all of the 100 x 20 x 6 different combinations have been made. Further variety is introduced because there is a second shorter section of DNA in the B cell that just has V and J combinations, and also by random base changes in the DNA sequence introduced in the manufacture process. Thus, from a relatively short length of chromosome, the body manufactures the vast numbers of slightly different B cells that are needed to fight off as yet unknown infections.

The orchestrated operation of the fifty trillion cells is not something that is learned as the body grows. All of the coding of the systems came from one single fertilised cell.

The Brain

Autopilot

Our brain also carries out many functions that we are not even aware of, in addition to our conscious thoughts. We are blissfully unaware of most of what is going on in our bodies. The operation of our cells happens automatically; each cell responding to stimuli that cross its boundary. Similarly most of our actions happen without our conscious awareness. We all know how difficult it is to take up a new activity, when we have to consciously cause our bodies to act in a given way. When I learned to touch type, it was agonisingly slow initially, slower than using one finger on each hand. But gradually I trained myself to be able to type satisfactorily using all my fingers, and at much higher speed. If you ask me today where each letter is on the keyboard I will struggle to tell you. My brain and body are best getting on with the job without my conscious help. However, when we are conscious we retain the ability to take control again and we can choose to be aware of what our body is up to.

Sleepwalkers have been known to do many tasks that one would imagine require conscious thought. These can be simple, like getting up and dressed, walking around, going to the bathroom, but also surprisingly complex tasks such as driving a car. Sleepwalkers will usually have their eyes open but they may have an expressionless face. They will not normally remember what they did when they wake up, and may be confused and disoriented when they wake.[56]

The body can operate equally with or without our consciousness. It's as if we have an autopilot. It appears possible to carry out the tasks of daily life without consciousness. We cannot therefore assume that people or animals are conscious as a result of observing what they do.

Brain Activity

Neuroscience is discovering that different areas of the brain are active when we carry out different functions.[57] By planting tiny electrodes in the brain, or by using MRI scanning techniques it is found that for instance, different accumulations of neurons are stimulated when the eye is presented with different images; a still scene rather than a moving scene. The brain seems organised in a tiered calculation system. There are special areas of the brain which

---

[56] http://www.ncbi.nlm.nih.gov/pubmedhealth/PMH0001811 accessed 8/7/13

[57] *God Soul Mind Brain: A Neuroscientist's Reflections on the Spirit World*, Michael S. A. Graziano, ISBN-10: 1935248111

become active when presented with something that looks like a face. Basic facial recognition seems to be hard wired, yet other less important objects do not. And there is another area that appears to pull all of the information together. This area interprets the model presented to it by the other processing parts of the brain and presents it in a way that is consciously understandable, allowing me to determine for instance that my wife's smile is a happy one.

Parts of our brain appear to mimic what we see others doing. The brain takes images of what others are doing and then runs them through its own higher tier calculation systems to try to understand what the other person is doing, thinking or feeling. We can indeed improve our sporting skills just by watching a game; our brain is practicing the same moves ready for next time we play. This helps us empathise or understand others, but it probably also helps us learn new skills.

There is data that suggests that consciousness may not occur at the same time that an event happens, but fractions of a second later[58]. Perhaps consciousness is not even instantaneous. When we listen to a sentence, we do not perceive each microsecond of the word as an isolated instant, we perceive the whole word, or even the sentence. When we listen to music, we don't just perceive an instantaneous note, we perceive the melody. It seems that we need to perceive over a window of time to be able to perceive at all.

---

[58] *Libet's Temporal Anomalies: A Reassessment of the Data* by Stanley A. Klein

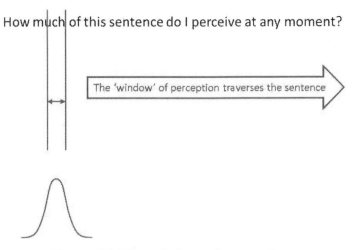

Figure 21. The window of perception

Our consciousness can interact with our memory, we can replay sounds that we've heard some time previously—we are aware that they are not in the present but we can still experience or "hear" them as precisely as when they occurred. Try it for yourself now. Drum your fingers on the table and then keep remembering the sound. You will find that you can remember it precisely and replay it in your consciousness.

With our consciousness we can focus our mind to solve problems. We can design tools, machines and complex systems, we can invent things. We can imagine things in the future that haven't happened yet. We can design things that haven't been thought of before. For example, take sixty seconds and list down all the uses you can think of for a coat-hanger. It's just a bit of bent wire, but we can think of many other things that we could do with it.

And we can imagine things that don't physically exist. We can do mathematics. We can write fantasy stories. We can imagine beautiful music and then write down a code to represent it. We can create works of art—we can interpret brush strokes on a canvas as a narrative of joy, pain, despair, according to what the artist intended.

We begin as a single cell and yet we end up with an amazingly complex processing unit called our brain.

Growth from a Single Cell

Each human begins as one cell, which divides a number of times to produce what is called a zygote. Initially each divided cell is the same as the others, but as the cells in the zygote continue to divide, cells begin to differ from each other. They start to develop the different parts of the body, although they may go through several transformations before reaching their final state.

The developing cell has immensely refined and complex control mechanisms to ensure that the right proteins are manufactured in the right order and at the right time for the cell to serve its function in the operation of the body. If they are not then the human will be deformed. Thalidomide taken at a particular time during pregnancy prevents certain steps in the developmental process happening, and so limbs don't form properly.[59]

Each cell is a self-contained entity. The only instructions that it can receive are signals that cross the cell membrane. The signals to do this pass from one cell to another. Not only does each individual cell have to know what to do in response to a signal from its neighbour, but it also has to pass on signals to its neighbour to allow that cell to perform its function too. It can only build with material that crosses the cell membrane.

Metamorphosis

The same development from a single egg to a full body operates in all animals, although some also go through a metamorphosis; tadpoles turn into frogs, caterpillars turn into butterflies. A tadpole has eyes on either side of its head, ideal for spotting a predator and fleeing for cover, yet when the tadpole becomes a frog the eyes have moved to the front of the head as required for a hunter. Not only have the eyes moved, but the nerve

---

[59] *Developmental Biology* (Eighth edition) Scott F Gilbert, ISBN 978-0-87893-250-4, P19

connections to the brain change too, allowing the frog to see stereoscopically, in three dimensions.[60]

During metamorphosis, the whole body adapts to be ready for the new environment that the organism will be living in. One of the most obvious changes is from the caterpillar to the butterfly. The caterpillar carries round dormant cells that will be activated later in life to form parts of the metamorphosed butterfly, whilst many of the cells which distinguish the caterpillar will die.

Salamander

Animals can have other features that are not present in humans. Salamanders have a remarkable self-repair mechanism. If you cut off the limb of a salamander, the wound will initially heal over into a stump. However, over time the cells in the stump begin to grow and to reform the amputated limb. The cells in the stump revert back to being stem cells (undifferentiated cells) and then the process of re-differentiation begins and proceeds until the new limb is formed.[61]

First Life

The human body, and indeed all plants and animals are extremely complex entities. The Theory of Evolution describes how complexity can be added from generation to generation, but says nothing about how life began.

3.8 billion years ago the earth contained the raw materials for life; the elemental molecules, the intermolecular forces, the prebiotic hydrocarbon molecules (amino acids, sugars, nitrogenous bases, phosphates). How did they transform into the life?

The earliest cells, such as the cyanobacteria that are found in the most ancient rocks, are already incredibly complex. How might life have existed before the cell? How did it begin?

---

[60] *Developmental Biology* (Eighth edition) Scott F Gilbert, ISBN 978-0-87893-250-4, P556

[61] *Developmental Biology* 8th Edition, Scott F Gilbert, ISBN 978-0-87893-250-4, page 574

The chemical processes in a cell are unlike other chemical processes where the reaction of the component molecules creates the target molecule spontaneously. The chemical reaction $H2 + O \Rightarrow H2O$ is straightforward and the output is different from the input; hydrogen and oxygen become water. Under the right conditions the reaction can also be reversed. However the output of living processes is a second copy of the input. The cell divides and produces two cells from one; it manufactures replicas of itself. This replication process is essential for life to have evolved. Therefore for life to begin we need a replicating molecule, or a series of molecules that replicate. But where would the first replicating molecules have come from? We either need one that originated spontaneously, or one that was manufactured by a non-replication process; a replicating molecule without a parent replicating molecule.

Replicating Molecules

Replicating molecules are complex, not at all like simple water or carbon dioxide molecules. It is accepted that life would not have begun with this full system of different types of molecules, but could it have begun with a single replicating molecule? Today the replication process requires a DNA molecule, polymerase and ribosome proteins and TRNA and MRNA molecules. The process uses DNA as the template to order the amino acids and make protein, and also needs protein enzymes to read and decode the DNA; it needs both DNA and protein enzymes.

It has been found experimentally that RNA can act as an enzyme, and it is of course very similar to DNA. It is hypothesised that at one time RNA acted as both template (like DNA) and enzyme (like protein). Perhaps an early form of life comprised replicating RNA alone; no DNA or proteins. This hypothesis is referred to as "RNA world."

The replication process must be sufficiently robust that there are at least as many successful offspring molecules as there were parent molecules. Does this work for RNA molecules?

In one experiment, a strand of RNA is placed in a solution of all of the constituent RNA bases. It is found that the RNA bases on the strand will pair with RNA bases from the solution, although the new bases are not linked together into a new strand. However, the pairing occurs without an enzyme. There is an error rate of around 1 in 20 in the pairing. In the presence of an enzyme, the accuracy of replication is shown experimentally to increase to over 1 in 1000.[62] Therefore to be able to replicate long molecules (over length of 20) it is necessary to have an enzyme.

In the RNA world, RNA needed to act as an enzyme. But the minimum length of RNA that allows it to act as an enzyme is around 40 nucleotides. GFJoyce and LE Orgel[63] write that:

> . . . *It is difficult to state with certainty the minimum possible size of an RNA replicase ribozyme. An RNA consisting of a single secondary structural element, that is a small stem-loop containing 12-17 nucleotides, would not be expected to have replicase activity, whereas a double stem-loop . . . might just be capable of a low level of activity. A triple stem-loop structure, containing 40-60 nucleotides, offers reasonable hope of functioning as a replicase ribozyme."*

For a robust replication process with a molecule of over 20 bases we need an enzyme, and yet the shortest RNA molecule that appears able to be an enzyme requires 40—60 bases. Something as yet unknown must have bridged that gap.

---

[62] *The Origins of Life* – John Maynard Smith and Eörs Szathmáry ISBN 019 850493 4 – p35

[63] *The RNA World - The Nature of Modern RNA Suggests a Prebiotic RNA* - 3 Rev Ed Raymond F. Gesteland, Editor: Thomas R. Cech, Editor: John F. Atkins Cold Spring Harbor Laboratory Press,U.S. (United States), 2005 ISBN-13: 9780879697396 page 32

Timeline

There are many well-established methods of methods for dating different rocks and fossil samples, and the best indicative timeline for the development of life on earth is as follows:

3.8 billion years ago: earth crust solidified.

3.5 billion years ago: fossil evidence of cellular cyanobacteria.

2 billion years ago sufficient free oxygen was produced to start to form the ozone layer and then to create an increasingly oxygen rich atmosphere.

1.5 billion years ago: first eukaryotic cells (cells with a nucleus) evident

1 billion years ago: first metaphytes (multicellular algae and higher plants)

500 million years ago: first metazoans (invertebrate and vertebrate animals)

1/4 million years ago: first homo-sapiens

5 billion years into the future: the earth is destroyed as the sun enters the red giant phase.

From the fossil records amongst the earliest cellular life on earth was cyanobacteria. Although these are relatively simple life-forms they are extremely resilient. They needed to be; the atmosphere was completely different to what it is today, and would be extremely hostile to almost all of today's life-forms. Cyanobacteria still live in an apparently unchanged form today, and remain extremely resilient. They can survive for prolonged periods of darkness, are highly resistant to X-rays, UV and gamma radiation. Some have survived extreme variations in temperature (-269 to 105°C), highly acidic and alkaline environment pH (2-10) [64] and some have survived within 1km of a nuclear explosion.

---

[64] "Tolerance of the widespread cyanobacterium Nostoc commune to extreme temperature variations (-269 to 105°C), pH and salt stress." Sand-Jensen K, Jespersen TS. Freshwater Biological Laboratory, Biological Institute, University of Copenhagen, Hillerød, Denmark. http://www.ncbi.nlm.nih.gov/pubmed/22120705 accessed 3/3/13

Cleaning the Atmosphere

Once cyanobacteria appeared on earth they carried out an essential function in preparing the earth for more complex life. For 1.5 to 2 billion years the cyanobacteria cleaned up the atmosphere and enriching it with oxygen, produced by photosynthesis. The effects can be seen geologically. Initially the released oxygen was used up by oxidising iron into rust and producing banded iron rock formations found in some of the oldest rocks. The oxygen was also absorbed into the oceans, and eventually enriched the atmosphere[65]. Only when there was a sufficiently oxygen rich atmosphere was it possible for more complex life to emerge.

Models of the development of the sun suggest that when cyanobacteria appeared the sun was only three quarters as bright as it is today. If the atmosphere during this "Archean period" was the same as it is today then the temperature on earth would have been too low for liquid water — it would have been a frozen planet. Of course, the initial cooling of the earth would have allowed water to remain liquid, but once that effect diminished it is thought that only the much higher concentration of greenhouse gases allowed the water to remain liquid[66]. Had the cyanobacteria worked too fast, removing the CO_2 from the atmosphere too quickly, then the water may have frozen and more complex life may not have developed.

In Conclusion

The biological sciences have shown that living things are made with incredibly complex systems of interacting molecules and chemistry. Cells are the building blocks of life, and the complex systems can only operate because they behave with intelligence; each cell knows what to do in a particular situation. Every living thing today began as a single cell. The scientific assumption is that the single cell contains all the capability to grow something as complex

---

[65] *Major Events in the History of Life.* J.William Schopf. ISBN 0-86720-268-8

[66] http://www.nature.com/scitable/knowledge/library/earth-s-earliest-climate-24206248 accessed 3/3/13

as a human being with no external input, and that the complexity increased and was consistently transmitted from generation to generation through the evolutionary process. Whether these assumptions are correct or not, we can be thankful to biologists for bringing to light what amazing bodies you and I inhabit.

If we want to know <u>why</u> we are here, we need to look further.

Chapter 3: The Universe Exhibits Design and Purpose

The last chapter described a lot of what science knows. This chapter starts to consider whether there are any hints or conclusions that might be drawn from the data. As a qualified design engineer, I conclude that the universe exhibits design and purpose. To understand why I reach that conclusion it is necessary to consider what design is, and whether design can exist without matter.

Design can certainly exist before the designed object comes into being; we design something before we make it. Humans have the capability to design things, to decide what something will look like before it is made. We don't randomly choose shapes for the pistons in our cars, and see which one works best; we look at the size of hole in the cylinder block and choose a piston to match. It is much faster and more efficient approach. We visualize and draw something before we make it, so that when we do make it we expect it to work first time.

However, although a designer will think of a particular design to solve a problem, the first design will seldom be the best. Through feedback of how the product works we improve and evolve the design. We may come up with many different design solutions for a given function, and then find out which works best. With the computer power available today it is possible to assess thousands or even millions of specific designs to come up with the best. In many cases we use a random approach to generate millions of slightly different designs that we then analyse to determine the optimum. All of this is design: designing the product itself, designing the process to generate the product design, designing the tools to analyse the product designs, and designing a way to determine which is best.

Using this approach we have developed tools and machines of extreme complexity. We started with the most rudimentary of tools, fashioned from sticks and stones. We used these tools to dig up metals and make simple metal tools. We used those simple tools to make more complex ones. And so on and so on. As our ancestors fashioned a primitive axe they didn't think that this was the first step towards a 52" plasma TV, but that is where our tool and machine evolutionary process has led.

An archaeologist from 2000 years in the future might look at today's tools (the motor car in the driveway for instance) and gradually dig up earlier and earlier tools. He might find all the steps in the evolutionary development of the tools right back to the first Stone Age axe. So would he be right to conclude that the tools had evolved? Yes. Would he be right to conclude that they had evolved through an un-designed and random process? Of course not. He would conclude that intelligent beings had designed the tools. He would conclude that 2000 years ago the essence of "Design" existed in the universe.

Take all the chemical constituents of the earth 3.8 billion years ago, add heat, light and gravitational forces from the sun and moon, and the odd meteorite, chance and the laws of physics. Stand back for 3.8 billion years. Take another look and we see the same set of chemicals, but now reconstructed into London, New York, trains, planes and automobiles, plasma TVs, the Internet, nuclear warheads, the complete works of Shakespeare, the Mona Lisa and so on, as well as a vast diversity of life. And of course we also find design and intelligence.

So was there a time when Design didn't exist in the universe? Was Design there at the Big Bang, or did it self-create some fourteen billion years into the process? Is there in fact any way of producing anything that is not by design, bearing in mind what Design actually is? It seems to me that the design that we carry out today and the design of the universe are compatible. Scientific discovery implies a mix of intentional design and of purposeful improvement through apparently random processes.

If we compare the rather primitive outcomes of our design ingenuity with the wonderful complexity of the human body, it seems perverse to claim that the primitive is designed and the complex is not.

The Continued Existence of the Universe.

The universe that exists today appears to operate in a predictable way, represented by the laws of physics which we try to model with equations. The equations usually include a number of constants. Models such as Einstein's theory of relativity match much of the measured data very well.

Some constants can be derived mathematically, such as the ratio of the circumference of a circle to the diameter which is known as Pi (the Greek letter π). Other constants are only obtained by careful measurement; we saw earlier how measurements of the speed of light changed over the years. There appears to be no reason why the speed of light is what it is, but its value is central to how the universe behaves.

We can do calculations with our models to see what might have happened if the constants had been different. This shows us that the constants in this universe seem to be incredibly fine-tuned. Indeed, if the constants were very different then the universe would not exist at all. John Lennox references theoretical physicist Paul Davies when he writes that:

> *if the ratio of the strong nuclear force to the electromagnetic force had been different by one part in 10^{16}, no stars could have formed. Again, the ratio of the electromagnetic force-constant to the gravitational force-constant must be equally delicately balanced. Increase it by only 1 part in 10^{40} and only small stars can exist; decrease it by the same amount and there will only be large stars. You must have both large and small stars in the universe; the large ones produce elements in their thermonuclear furnaces and it is only the small ones that burn long enough to sustain a planet with life. . . . that is the*

kind of accuracy a marksman would need to hit a coin on the far side of the observable universe, twenty billion light years away. [67]

and also

The periodic table of elements would look different with a changed strong nuclear force. If it were weaker there would be fewer stable chemical elements. The more complex organisms require about twenty-seven chemical elements, iodine being the heaviest (with an atomic number of 53). Instead of ninety- two naturally occurring elements, a universe with a strong force weaker by 50% would have contained only about twenty to thirty. This would eliminate the life-essential elements iron and molybdenum.[68]

If these constants are indeed not mathematically derivable then it does seem extremely fortuitous that they are what they are, which begs the question: "Why are the constants what they are?"

Whilst science cannot answer this question it is not irrefutable proof of a designer. If the values of the constants were different then we would not be here, able to measure them. Everything is like it is; otherwise it would simply be different. This sort of thinking is referred to as the Anthropic Principle. We are only able to observe the fine tuning because we need fine tuning in order to exist as an observer.

Unlikely Events Do Happen

We cannot take extremely unlikely events in the universe as definitive proof that the universe is designed and so needs a designer. Extremely unlikely things do happen. Derren Brown was filmed tossing a coin ten times in a row and each time the coin turned up

---

[67] *John C. Lennox: God's Undertaker – Has Science Buried God?* ISBN 978-0-7459-5371-7

[68] *John C. Lennox: God's Undertaker – Has Science Buried God?* ISBN 978-0-7459-5371-7

heads. The chances of that are 1000 to 1 against. Is he just extremely lucky? No, he did it by tossing the coin lots and lots of times until it happened. It may have taken a long time to film the sequence, but it made good TV. The point is, if you have enough tries, then the extremely unlikely can happen.

The implication with regard to our universe is that either this is the only universe that has ever come into existence, and it has been fine-tuned, or there are an incredibly large number of universes that have come into existence with different sets of physical laws and constants. This is the multiverse theory, and is of course outside of the realm of science; it is not amenable to experiment, proof or disproof.

Since there is no reason to limit the number of alternative universes, multiverse theory must imply that there are an infinite number. The vast majority of these other universes will have different constants and laws to ours but we would also suppose that there are other universes with exactly the same constants as ours.

> **Hypothesis contrary to fact**
>
> One can look at this as speculation, or sometimes wishful thinking. If "this" hadn't happened then "that" would have happened, or "this" only happened because of "that." For example, "If I'd had a better Science teacher I'd have become a scientist." Or "If I'd married someone else then I'd be happier."

Whilst some may claim that multiverse theory removes the possibility of a God, we should quickly realise that it does no such thing. Even if there are an infinite number of universes the question remains of how and why the infinite number of universes came into being.

It is interesting to note that the earth is in a particularly favourable position from which to observe the universe. If the earth were in an average solar system closer to the middle of the galaxy, we would not get such a good view of the universe. Our sky would be much brighter due to the larger number of nearby stars, and we would not be able to deduce things like the universe having a beginning; we wouldn't be able to measure the background radiation that helped lead us to that conclusion. Applying multiverse theory would tell us that there must be many universes with the same physical constants, where life has developed, and where the living creatures are not on a planet in the ideal position to observe and learn about the universe. To me, this is stretching the multiverse theory a little far, and suggest that it is more than just co-incidence that the one planet that we know has life is in the ideal situation for an advanced form of life (us) to observe the remainder of the universe and begin to understand some of the wonder of it. It's almost as if someone wants us to find out.

Quantum Physics

There is weirdness at the quantum level and unpredictability in the behaviour of individual particles, but there seems to be predictability when you put them all together. Our equations hint at an understanding that seems almost within our grasp, but there remains a screen beyond which we cannot look — the behaviour of an individual particle.

Even to formulate the mathematical equations to describe what happens scientists have used what is called Hilbert Space[69], a non-physical realm where the state of a particle can be represented by a vector in an imaginary world. In the imaginary world the vectors are manipulated by operators (corresponding to observations in the real world).

It seems that something that is not constrained by rigid laws "decides" how each single particle behaves in the two slit experiment, and yet ensures that the behaviour of a large number of particles is consistent and predictable.

---

[69] *Quantum Theory* – John Polkinghorne, ISBN 0-19-280252-6 p27

This addresses some of the difficulties that religious scientists might have had in Newton's days. If Newtonian physics was correct then it is impossible to conceive of a mechanism whereby a God can influence events. In a Newtonian universe, once everything has been set rolling then all events in the future are already determined by the laws of physics. There can be no such thing as free will or even chance. In such a universe it is impossible to see for example how prayer might work without breaking the determined laws of physics.

However, the behaviour of subatomic particles shows us that it is totally reasonable to believe that God can answer prayer in a manner fully consistent with our discoveries of physics; God could choose where any individual particle ends up on the wall behind the two slits, but also ensure that the interference pattern is consistently obtained.

Similarly, the demonstrated mechanism of quantum entanglement implies that the course of events in one place can immediately be known in another; it is reasonable that God can know what is happening everywhere in the universe without having to break the laws of physics.

How to Engineer a Human

The human body (and all other animals and plants) look like incredibly complicated machines. Indeed, some scientists and philosophers do indeed consider them to be machines. Others look at the complexity and conclude that they must have been designed, and so infer a designer—God. They argue that the complexity of life is proof that there must be a God. I am a Chartered Engineer and challenged by the complexity of the biological machinery I decided to a look at how a designer today might go about engineering a human being. In the back of my mind is the question "Could it have been done any other way?"

I'll start by looking at the typical design and engineering process used today.

The Design Phase

The design and manufacture process today is a complex, multi-disciplined endeavour requiring careful planning and execution.

At 100% design release of the Boeing 747-8I the engineering team was reported to have completed a total of about 10,600 drawings for the new aircraft.[70] That number probably doesn't include the detailed drawings and design calculations necessary for each of the components. The jet engines for example were probably only represented by their interfaces to the aircraft wing, and would have had a set of their own drawings and design definitions.

In round numbers, those drawings probably described around 10,000 components. Let's guess that the development cost of the aircraft was around half a billion dollars. A rule of thumb is that one man-year costs 100 thousand dollars, and so the aircraft would have needed about 5000 man years to design, and hence each component would take about half a man-year to design. That estimate assumes all of the pre-existing know-how that the engineers will have gained from designing earlier aircraft.

However, the amount of design time per component increases with the complexity of the overall machine. The complexity goes up exponentially with the number of components. It would not take one and a half man years to design a pair of scissors comprising just 3 components for example. A human is far more complex than a Boeing 747-8I, and so if we were to use conventional engineering methods then one can imagine that the design time per component would be much higher.

Specialists

The complexity of the design of an aircraft is such that no individual can do it all. There are specialists in many areas:

---

[70] http://www.flightglobal.com/news/articles/farnborough-boeing-presses-on-with-747-8-certification-effort-343869/ Accessed 1/4/13

- Geometric design
- Aerodynamic analysis
- Stress analysis
- Material selection
- Heat transfer analysis
- Integration and system design
- Start up and operation
- Manufacturing

And there are further sub-specialists in each of these areas. It is all too much for one brain, and so the chief designer will break down the overall activity into smaller task. For instance, he might give the task "design the seat mounting" to a team. That team will have to determine the requirements of the seat mounting, what components it interfaces with, when it is needed in the assembly process and so on. The team will then carry out the design of the mounting. The team will also understand something of the overall design and operation of the aircraft even if they are not required to do anything with most of that knowledge. But they will for instance need to know how quickly the aircraft will accelerate in order to determine the likely forces to transmit to the seat and hence to the passenger.

In essence, each person on the team knows what they need to do and the context in which they are doing it. They will work within the "Standards" of the project such as the use of metric units of measurement. The team will know the required schedule for their activities; when can they start, and when do they need to finish the design of their component. Each person on the team will bring their engineering skills and know-how to the project, and can then be trusted to get on with their own task, although often a supervisor or colleague will check their work.

Optimisation

Each component needs to be optimised for its task. For a small component, the optimisation will be carried out using the inventiveness and technical know-how of the designer. He will know that a given material can withstand a given stress, and he can calculate the shape needed to carry the required load without exceeding that stress. He may try a few different geometric shapes in order to determine the optimum.

However, as the design problem becomes more complex, the number of options becomes too great to be sure that pure "know-how" on the part of the designer will lead to the optimum. Design optimisation is essentially an educated trial-and-error process, where for simple systems the "educated" part is adequate, but for more complex systems there needs to be some automation of the "trial-and-error" part.

The first step in such automation is the creation of mathematical simulations of the component which are then coded into a computer program to allow a large number of alternatives to be assessed in a short timescale. Since the generation of the design to be assessed is generally quite time-consuming, a design will usually be defined by a few parameters. For examining the aerodynamic performance of an aircraft wing the parameters might be: the length, the thickness distribution from fuselage to tip, the aerofoil type (from previously defined families of standard aerofoil shapes), the sweep, whether it is above or below the fuselage, the position along the length of the fuselage.

For just those six parameters we can see that there are a massive number of possible combinations that one could assess, and so the engineers will tend to find out which are the most important parameters and select the best of those, and then start to optimise the least important parameters. So for instance, he might quickly identify that the optimum position for the wing is underneath and half way along the fuselage. He may then determine the optimum sweep and length, and finally the thickness distribution (which will depend on both strength and aerodynamic requirements) and the aerofoil family.

Described like that it sounds much more manageable, but nevertheless we still see quite a variety of aircraft designs so we don't appear to have converged on a single optimum design. Competitive pressure ensures that sub-optimal designs are rarely seen, but there is scope for several successful variants.

Defining the Optimum

One of the most difficult aspects of the design optimisation process is to determine what functionality makes a design optimum. For instance, overall design parameters to be optimised for a particular aircraft will include:

- The range
- The fuel efficiency
- The speed
- The cost
- The manufacture time
- The number of seats
- The take-off and landing airstrip length
- Engine noise

Unfortunately it is not possible to have the maximum of each parameter. For maximum fuel efficiency you will want a lower speed, and lowest weight. Lightweight materials push up the cost, and adding more seats increases the weight. Clearly a trade-off between the different functions is required, and part of the success of a given design depends on what balance of parameters is selected during the concept phase of the design. Engineers are continually seeking better ways to optimise designs in the multi-parameter design space.

Optimum Operation.

Once the design is complete, the operational parameters also need to be optimised. Take a different example, a complex chemical plant. There are many interconnected components (storage tanks with level and pressure controllers, pumps, valves, interconnecting pipework, turbines, heaters, coolers etc.). It is standard practice to create an analytical model of the complete plant to simulate how it will respond, but the difficulty comes in deciding how to optimise operation of the plant. At the design stage it is necessary to select the right components; how large should the tank be, what type of valve are needed etc. For an operational plant it is necessary to tune the control characteristics for each component. If the fluid level in a tank drops, how quickly should the inlet valve open in order to maintain the level of the tank without overshooting and without disrupting the operation of the upstream components?

To do this by hand is time-consuming and it may be difficult enough for the designer to ensure that the plant actually works, let alone optimising the operation. To investigate the vast number of alternative combinations of settings would be impossible. With only twenty variables to choose from and only two settings for each, the possible number of combinations exceeds one million. It is clearly impractical to try to optimise these by trial and error. The saving grace is that not all of the parameters are particularly dependent on each other, for example the optimum value for parameter number 12 might always be 3, whatever the value of all the other parameters. Complex mathematical algorithms are used to improve the speed and quality of these optimisations.

Manufacture

Once designed, the product goes into the manufacture phase. There are two main aspects of manufacture; making the components and assembling them together.

In order to make a given component you start with the raw materials and then manipulate them in various different ways. For instance, the seat bracket might be made by casting aluminium into the basic shape of the bracket, then machining the surfaces of the bracket that join with the fuselage and with the seat itself, and finally machining the bolt holes and threads to allow the seat to be fitted securely to the fuselage.

All of the components need to be assembled in the right order. A mistake that inexperienced engineers sometimes make is to design superb components that simply cannot be assembled. You can assemble a ship in a bottle, but only if you design and make the ship with great ingenuity and skill. Teams of engineers can spend years working out the schedule to assemble an expensive design in a short period of time. Once you have bought all the components for your Boeing 747 you don't want them sitting in the stores for long. You want that plane out of the door and sold to the customer.

In a large engineering project the order of assembly of each component will be carefully specified to ensure that the right component is put in the right position at the right time in the process. However, the assembly team are always left to work out the fine details. They won't need to be told how to pick up a bolt and screw it into a hole, they will know from experience or common sense.

> **Logical fallacy: Hasty generalisation**
>
> This is drawing a conclusion based on too little evidence, or too small a sample. Of course, it can often be a matter of opinion about how big a sample is required to draw a conclusion, depending on the mechanics of the issue being addressed.

Estimating the Task of Designing a Human

At the start of any major project, engineers will make estimates of the amount of time and cost to complete the project. These will be based on past experience and an incomplete knowledge of what the final project will look like, and as such they will always be wrong, but normally not too far wrong. For an innovative project, a rule of thumb is to multiply your estimate by a factor of three. We do tend to be over-optimistic. So how long might it take to design a human?

The human has fifty trillion cells. Each cell is far more complex than each of the components in an airliner, but ignoring that for a moment, if we apply our rule of thumb of half a man-year to design each component, using the best engineers around today it would take us twenty-five trillion man years to design a human. But remember that design time per component tends to increase with complexity of the overall system design and so in practice we would have to estimate that it would take very much longer.

DNA is Not Enough

Is it really possible that all the information necessary to grow and operate fifty trillion different cells over the entire lifespan of a human is fully encoded in the DNA of the original single cell? Is there really enough information in that first cell to construct the wonder of the brain? As Susan Aldridge comments:

> *Powerful as it is, it is unlikely that DNA alone can explain why we have discovered its secrets and their potential to meet human needs!* [71]

In order to define the position of each cell we would need at least fifty trillion data items, one for each cell (Cell "A" is at position "x"). We may need more data since not only does each cell need to be in the right place, but also in the right orientation. In human DNA there are 3 billion base pairs; characters that we can use to define the positions. Even if we used one base pair to define the position of each cell we are 10,000 time too short of information carrying capacity in the DNA.

But it's worse than that. In the DNA base pair system of numbering the letters CAGT are equivalent to numbers in base 4. In base 10, the number fifty trillion (50,000,000,000,000) uses eleven characters, but in base 4 we would need 23 characters. Our 3,000,000,000 DNA base pairs can only now specify 150,000,000 positions—300,000 times less than we need to define the position of each cell.

If we put all of the onus on the DNA, then in addition to the position and type of cell, we are asking the DNA to carry the information to define the construction sequence and to program all of our behaviour patterns, our "operating system."

---

[71] *The Thread of Life* - Susan Aldridge – ISBN 0 521 46542 7 – page 251

But do I need to define the precise position of each cell? I'll explore that with an example.

Reconstructing London Bridge

Some years ago the City of London sold London Bridge to a rich American. Rumour has it that he thought he'd bought Tower Bridge, but that's another story. Anyway, London Bridge was duly dismantled and shipped to America where it was reassembled. Each brick and feature was carefully disassembled and numbered, and the position of each brick was recorded so that when the bridge was reassembled each part was in exactly the right place. For that process you would need one number for each component.

Figure 22. Reconstructed London Bridge in Lake Havasu, Arizona. (by Aran Johnson)

However, when the bridge was first built there would have been some parts of the bridge (flat surfaces for instance) where the designer would simply have instructed the craftsmen building it to put blocks to make a flat surface, he wouldn't have defined each block. But once the bridge had been built then the size and shape of each block was defined—partly by the designer and partly by the craftsmen building it. If any block was damaged, it would need to be replaced with a block of the identical size and shape in order to complete the repair. So to dismantle and reassemble the bridge, the complete definition of each component would need to be recorded and repeated when the bridge was rebuilt.

If we look at our hand we see intricate junctions of skin and fingernails, hair follicles and hardened pads. We see wrinkled skin over the joints of our fingers and folds in the skin on our palms. We see fingerprints whose shape doesn't change throughout our life. They are all skin cells, but each cell is in a precise position and of a precise type. To take our hand and specify the design needs a vast amount of information. But is this like the example of London Bridge? Perhaps it is not necessary for our DNA to define the precise position of each cell, but instead to allow the hand to determine the details as it develops. If we compare identical twins we see that growth from the same first cell produces very similar but not completely identical results. Would that happen if DNA contained the complete definition of the human?

But if DNA is not just a set of blueprints that by themselves define a human being, what *is* going on?

In the same way that an assembly instruction in the manufacture of the Boeing747-8i might say "assemble the following five components" and rely on the assembly team to know how to do it, maybe DNA contains an instruction that says "manufacture a toenail" and then the cell has to figure out how to do it. What if the cells are intelligent components that know what to do and simply get on with the task?

Intelligent Components

From experiments entailing bombarding fruit flies with radiation to change their DNA we see changes in the shape of the fruit fly. It is found that a single change in the DNA leads to a big change in the shape of the fly. A single mutation causes the position of all the cells in the wing to be redefined. The cells in the fruit fly seem to know that the single change in the DNA means "change the shape of the wing," and so they simply get on and do the job.

When we engineer and manufacture things today we need an intelligent workforce that is able to act on simplified instructions and carry out a complex manufacturing task. The body comprises many cells, each of which contains a set of instructions. That set of instructions cannot be enough to define the body, so we can infer that each cell has some intelligence of its own; it must have more knowledge than can be contained in the DNA. The cells are an intelligent workforce.

But the cell doesn't have a brain, where does it get its intelligence?

The cell membrane has many proteins embedded within it that can either respond or not to a stimulus from the outside world. This is rather like an "if-then" statement in a computer program, "if this molecule is present then tell the internals of the cell." So the cell membrane seems a good candidate for providing some of the intelligence required.

But the proteins in the cell membrane are manufactured by the cell, or by a parent of the cell—how did they know which proteins to manufacture for the offspring cell? Following this sequence of requirements back, we must end up with the first cell, which "knows" exactly what offspring cells to manufacture in order to start the complete and complex sequence that ends with the fully formed human being. This seems to put a very heavy a requirement on the first cell. I wonder if there is more intelligence than that which is hard coded by the various protein gates embedded in the cell membrane. Is there something else sustaining or guiding the growth?

Amoeba

Amoebas are single-celled organisms that demonstrate intelligence. They have no brain but they behave in a purposeful way; they catch and eat their prey. It is interesting to note that the amoeba proteus has 290 billion base pairs in its DNA, compared to humans who have a mere 2.9 billion. This reinforces the idea that the DNA does not contain all of the required information; why would a single-celled amoeba need more information than a human being?

Controlling the Schedule

There is no point in putting the gas turbine engine on the wing of the Boeing747-8i if the turbine blades have not yet been assembled into the engine, so in engineering we have to define the assembly sequence, and then tell the assembly team when to start different tasks. Signals can be used to define the start of different phases in the construction. King Henry V didn't give each of his archers an individual instruction to fire on the French at Agincourt, a single instruction would be understood by them all. An archer that didn't hear the order would join in anyway by seeing what was happening around him. And when they ran out of arrows they knew without being told that they had to use their swords for hand to hand fighting. We see this sort of signalling instruction being given in the human body too; a single hormone released into the bloodstream tells many cells around the body to carry out many different tasks. Again this is demonstrating a form of intelligence in the cells—they know what to do as a result of the general instruction.

Intelligent Optimisation

In the design of an aircraft there are components which are able to change in order to accommodate the different conditions during different parts of the flight. The rudder moves to adjust the yaw of the plane if there is a side wind, the engines produce more power to accelerate the plane. There are dynamically active components such as the rudder, but there are also one-off changes such as extending the wings during landing to give greater lift at low speed. And on the ground it is possible to make other changes if the duty of the plane changes; for instance removing the seats if the plane has to handle cargo. Each of these changes required intelligence and forethought to design and implement the changes. But imagine a wing that is made of intelligent components which sense the speed and direction of the wind and by themselves change shape to match it. Imagine a wing strut that makes itself thicker if it finds that it is operating with too high stress. Imagine a machine which is able to optimise itself. We can see that such a machine become possible with intelligent components, and that's what we have with the body: we have bones that change their shape to minimise the stresses, muscles that grow when they find that they are not strong enough. We have a body comprising intelligent components that operate without conscious control from their "pilot."

With the application of intelligent components it becomes possible to minimise the information needed to define the machine. The components themselves can optimise their operation according to their environment without having to be told by a central controller. More and more intelligent components are being used today in our machines, local microprocessors controlling the operation of distributed components in response to an environmental change or an instruction from the master controller. But the human body is many times better at doing this; each cell is like the microprocessor. But each cell is also a self-manufacturing component. To one skilled in the art of engineering, this is brilliant design!

The Only Way?

Would it be possible to design a human being in any other way? It seems to me that unless each human being, each plant and animal was individually manufactured using tools and processes external to the organism itself it is essential to embed some form of intelligence in each of the components. I suspect that if DNA did indeed contain all the necessary information to define a human, then it would simply be too long to fit within the cell, and it would still need some form of decoder.

But if the cells are intelligent components, is the intelligence simply provided by the membrane of the cell? I can't help thinking of the phrase that is found in Psalm 139 in the Bible :

> You made all the delicate, inner parts of my body and knit me together in my mother's womb. Thank you for making me so wonderfully complex! Your workmanship is marvellous—how well I know it. You watched me as I was being formed in utter seclusion, as I was woven together in the dark of the womb.

The Unlikely Origin of Life

Richard Dawkins in a discussion on the origin of life with Rowan Williams and Anthony Kenny[72] commented that

> *"Self-replicating molecules that made copies of themselves came into existence by sheer luck. . . . Nobody knows how it happened."*

But as we know, lucky things can happen if you try long enough. Indeed Dawkins commented that there are perhaps 10^{22} planets in the universe, which sounds a pretty big number of chances.

But how does that compare with the number of attempts that sheer luck might need to produce a self-replicating molecule?

We learned earlier that in RNA world we needed RNA with 40 bases in order for it to act as an enzyme. If the only mechanism for the 40 bases to assemble were sheer luck then this turns out to be an extremely unlikely event. Joyce and Orgel note that

> *If two or more copies of the same 40 (base) RNA are needed, then a much larger library, consisting of 10^{48} RNAs and weighing 10^{28}g, would be required. This amount is comparable to the mass of the earth.*[73]

In other words, if their assumptions and calculations are correct, the likelihood of the spontaneous creation of RNA is the same as searching for a single molecule in the whole mass of the earth.

If we think of each of the 10^{22} planets in the universe as another opportunity for the unlikely event to occur, it would reduce

---

[72] "Nature of human beings and the question of their ultimate origin" - Debate at the Sheldonian Theatre, Oxford, February 23rd 2012 with Prof Richard Dawkins, Archbishop of Canterbury Dr Rowan Williams and Philosopher Sir Anthony Kenny

[73] "The RNA World - The Nature of Modern RNA Suggests a Prebiotic RNA" - 3 Rev Ed Raymond F. Gesteland, Editor: Thomas R. Cech, Editor: John F. Atkins Cold Spring Harbor Laboratory Press,U.S. (United States), 2005 ISBN-13: 9780879697396 page 32

the staggering improbability (1 in 10^{48}) of such a molecule occurring somewhere in the universe to an only slightly less staggering improbability of 1 in 10^{26}. Only multiverse theory can explain how sheer luck might lead to life occurring on one of them, and with an infinite number of multiverses the chance becomes certainty. And then we just happen to be in one of the universes where life occurred. We could not be on a planet or in a universe where life didn't occur, by definition, because we are alive; the Anthropic Principle again.

However, I wonder if the probability of the initiation of life is indeed as low as noted above. It seems that the matter in the universe and the laws of physics that maintain it are perfectly designed for the generation and evolution of life. We are about to see that the rate of evolutionary change is very fast, and it seems that the characteristics of the chemistry are ideally favourable to the whole process. It would not be surprising if that same chemistry were not tilted to strongly favour initiation of life itself. A blind golfer is unlikely to putt the ball into the hole, unless the putting green is funnelled in such a way as to guide the ball into the hole. Perhaps like the golfer we are blind to the slope on the green.

The only thing that we know for certain about the origin of life on this planet is that there was one. Four billion years ago there was no life on earth, three and a half billion years ago there was. And five billion years into the future, the earth will be swallowed up by the sun as it enters the red giant phase.

The Speed and End of Evolution

How Many Generations

The timeline at the end of chapter 2 shows that it took at maximum 300 million years for cyanobacteria, an already very complex life-form, to appear on earth. This discovery was a surprise to me. The age of the universe (14 billion years) or of the earth (4.5 billion years) is often cited as the time available for evolution. Another surprise was that it took only 500 million years for multicelled life to develop into the incredibly complex life-form that is us today.

Since evolution progresses by the transmission of changes from one generation to the next, it is interesting to consider the number of generations of different types of life.

Bacteria typically reproduce every hour, so in the 3.5 billion years since cyanobacteria first emerged there have been about 35 trillion generations. There seems to have been little evolutionary change in the 2 billion years before the first cells with a nucleus appeared.

Animals first emerged around 500 million years ago, and with a typical generation of 2 years implying around 250million generations to move from the first animals to one with all of the complexity that we see in a human. Humans emerged only 250 thousand years ago, with a mere twelve thousand generations for evolutionary changes to take place.

	Typical generation	Time since first fossil evidence	Total number of generations since first fossil evidence
bacteria	1 hour (~ 10000 per year)	3.5 billion (3.5 x 10^9) years	35 trillion (3.5 x 10^{13})
animals	2 years	500 million (5 x 10^8) years	250 million (2.5 x 10^8)
humans	22 years	250 thousand (2.5 x 10^5) years	12 thousand

It seems to me that this data shows that the origin of life and the evolutionary changes that we've seen since the origin has actually taken place surprisingly quickly. Two hundred and fifty million generations (iterations) to refine a human being from a primitive animal does not seem that many. With only twenty variables, each with only two settings, the possible number of combinations exceeds one million. Complexity increases exponentially, and so forty variables with four alternative settings would give a possible number of combinations of 10^{24} compared with which 2.5×10^8 or even 3.5×10^{13} generations are remarkably small numbers. As we saw earlier, humans are exceedingly complex systems, built from intelligent components which derive from a first single cell.

The efficiency of the process when understood in the context of the engineering required to produce complex and optimised systems demonstrates that the process of evolution cannot simply be random. There is something about this universe which has ensured that the process was inevitable. Brian Cox remarked in his TV documentary series that there

> "... must be a non-random element to evolution, a natural process which greatly restricts this universe of possibilities and shapes the outcome." [74]

He asserts that the non-random element is natural selection. Whilst I agree that natural selection will select the most successful from a given population it begs the question of where the population came from, and so of itself must be an incomplete mechanism. And it seems to me that the scale of the task is orders of magnitude too big.

Of course, no optimisation process would laboriously plod through each of the possible combinations in order to reach the solution. The natural selection process eliminates a large number of possible combinations at each generation, but since the size of the

---

[74] *Wonders of Life – Endless Forms Most Beautiful* – first broadcast 10/2/13

problem increases exponentially with increased complexity ten trillion iterations perhaps isn't such a large number.

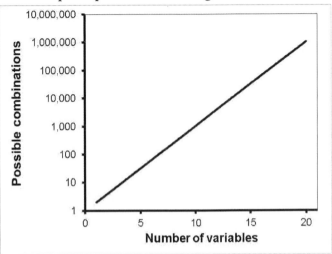

Figure 23. Combination increase with number of variables

The Intelligent Design (ID) movement attempts to quantify the unlikelihood of evolution being a chance process. Unfortunately the movement overstates their case scientifically, and politically they want ID to be considered science, and have thus encountered scepticism and scorn from the establishment. However I would recommend reading some of what they publish.[75][76]

The core of the argument is that the chance of life occurring in an un-guided and un-designed process is so remote as to be impossible, yet life has occurred and so this indicates that there must be a designer.

Satanic Leaf-Tailed Gecko

In Madagascar there is a fascinating lizard, the Satanic Leaf-Tailed Gecko (*Uroplatus phantasticus*). This little lizard has evolved to look almost exactly like a dead leaf (see picture). It has perfect colouring, and even has little nicks in the tail to look like a leaf that has been eaten by caterpillars. There are many variables to optimise

---

[75] *The Edge of Evolution* Dr Michael Behe ISBN 978-0-7432-9622-9
[76] *Signature in the Cell* Stephen C. Meyer ISBN 978-0-06-147278-7

in developing this particular gecko (colour, size, texture, shape of head, tail, nicks in the tail etc.) and so a vast number of combinations. With only 250 million generations since the first fossil evidence of animals, is it possible for a process that relies on sheer luck to lead to such a perfect match? The absolute precision of the gecko in mirroring the leaf is so astonishing that it hints of intentionality in its development.

Figure 24. Satanic Leaf-Tailed Gecko

Convergent Evolution

There are other strong hints that the evolutionary process maybe following a purpose, or is designed to seek a particular goal. The camera eye has evolved on many occasions through very different evolutionary paths to an almost identical design. This is called convergent evolution.

The octopus and human eye evolved independently, yet the design and functionality is almost identical, with only a minor difference in that the octopus eye does not have the blind spot on the retina where the optic nerve connects to the nerves in the eye.

> *The camera eye has actually evolved at least seven times, most extraordinarily in a group of jellyfish known as the box-jellies (or cubozoans). Although these jellyfish have a nervous system, they don't have a brain, and furthermore they belong to a phylum known*

as cnidarians, widely agreed to be amongst the most primitive of animals.[77]

The pill bug and the pill millipede have very similar structure, and yet the pill bug is actually a class of woodlouse.

Figure 25. Example of evolutionary convergence

These are two of many examples of convergence on a common solution, via different evolutionary routes. This suggests that the outcome of the evolutionary process may be predetermined. Perhaps there is a predefined or intrinsic set of perfect organisms within the universe and the mechanisms of evolution are simply the means of progressing towards that perfection. The precise route may not be defined, but the end goal or purpose is.

---

[77]http://www.mapoflife.org/about/convergent_evolution/?section=0 accessed 3/3/13

In Conclusion

Does Darwinian evolution have anything to say about God or no God? It is interesting that Darwin's book is called *On the Origin of Species*, not *On the Origin of Life*, and in his final paragraph he refers to "several powers, having been originally breathed into a few forms or into one"[78]. Clearly he understood evolution to be completely consistent with the existence of God. For those who struggle with evolution and creation today, molecular biologist and Christian, Dennis Alexander demonstrates that evolution is fully consistent with Christianity.[79]

Earlier I quoted John Maynard Smith and Eörs Szathmáry:

> . . . *six unique transitions, together with the origins of life itself, which we also think to have been a unique sequence of events. Any one of them might not have*

---

[78] *On the Origin of Species By Means of Natural Selection, or, the Preservation of Favoured Races in the Struggle for Life* by Charles Darwin, 1859

[79] *Creation or Evolution, do we have to choose?* Dennis Alexander ISBN 978-1-85424-746-9

happened, and if not, we would not be here, nor any
organism remotely like us. [80]

The fact that there have been *"six unique transitions"* which might not have happened, the convergence of many evolutionary routes on similar designs, and the speed at which the evolutionary process has achieved its results all seem to me to be indicative of, or at least consistent with a goal or purpose to the universe.

---

[80] *The Origins of Life* – John Maynard Smith and Eörs Szathmáry ISBN 019 850493 4 - p18-19

Chapter 4: Not Everything Can Be Explained by Science.

At school, I learned that science can explain everything, and that there was no need for the outdated idea of God. I now know that either I misunderstood, or I was badly taught. This isn't a claim that science itself makes; science does not claim to explain everything. But "Scientism" does.

> *Scientism is a philosophical position that exalts the methods of the natural sciences above all other modes of human inquiry. . . . Such a doctrinaire stance associated with science leads to an abuse of reason that transforms a rational philosophy of science into an irrational dogma.*[81]

Proponents of scientism endeavour to prove that science is sufficient, that there is no need of God, and that there is no God. In the doctrine of scientism there is no possibility of agreeing with the conclusion being discussed in this chapter. But let's begin by looking at what science claims for itself.

What is Science?

"What is science?" It's not as straightforward a question as one might think. The UK Science Council spent a year coming up with a definition:

> *Science is the pursuit of knowledge and understanding of the natural and social world following a systematic methodology based on evidence.*[82]

They are quite pleased with this and comment on their website as follows:

---

[81]http://carbon.ucdenver.edu/~mryder/scientism_este.html accessed 10/6/13

[82] http://www.sciencecouncil.org/definition accessed 11/3/13

Why define science?

The Science Council has "science" in its name but had not previously clarified what this actually meant. In addition to developing a better understanding of what types of organisations might become member bodies, it was felt that the recent inclusion of the advancement of science as a charitable activity in the 2006 Charities Act suggested that in that context a definition would be useful; and finally, the Science Council agreed that it wanted to be clearer when it talked about sound science and science based policy what it was actually describing.

Scientific methodology includes the following:

Objective observation: Measurement and data (possibly although not necessarily using mathematics as a tool)

Evidence

Experiment and/or observation as benchmarks for testing hypotheses

Induction: reasoning to establish general rules or conclusions drawn from facts or examples

Repetition

Critical analysis

Verification and testing: critical exposure to scrutiny, peer review and assessment

When we looked into this we found that definitions of science were not readily available, and were not easily accessible on the Internet.

Leading philosopher A C Grayling commended the Science Council's definition

"Because 'science' denotes such a very wide range of activities a definition of it needs to be general; it certainly needs to cover investigation of the social as well as natural worlds; it needs the words 'systematic' and 'evidence'; and it needs to be simple and short. The definition succeeds in all these respects admirably, and I applaud it therefore"

Science relies on the <u>assumption</u> that everything works according to fixed laws (the requirement for repetition in the scientific methodology described above). The goal of science is to try to determine those laws. Scientists can then create models based on the laws which make predictions which can be compared with measurements. In general, a new theory is only accepted when the majority agree that the model fits the experiments. New ideas and models are subject to scrutiny and peer review.

For something to become scientific knowledge, it has to be sufficiently predictable and repeatable. Something that doesn't happen repeatably is by definition outside the realm of science.

Measurement Beats Theory

Science attempts to describe how real things behave in terms of the formulae and equations, but we must be careful not to believe the equations over reality. Newton was convinced that his theory of gravity was perfect; it predicted extremely accurately the motion of almost all of the solar system. When some discrepancies were noticed in the motion of Uranus, Newton's gravitational theory was used to predict the existence and position of Neptune before it was discovered. When the orbit of Mercury was found to be different from what was predicted it was thought once again that there were other bodies in the solar system that had not been observed yet which were causing the discrepancy. It was only when Einstein's theory of relativity gave a slightly different prediction which accurately matched the measurement that the idea of extra bodies was abandoned and it was agreed that Newton's model had been inaccurate. Interestingly, we seem to be in a similar situation today.

The behaviour of distant galaxies differs from what is predicted by relativity, and scientists have deduced the existence of "Dark Matter" to balance the equations.[83] Is Newton's mistake being repeated?

The Science Council definition of science notes that objective observation is necessary for science. However this presents some difficulties. It is impossible to make observations of particular events such as the formation of the earth or the origin of life. And importantly, the observation of something often causes a change in its behaviour. We can measure the strength of a substance by stretching it to breaking point, but by doing so we have destroyed its strength. We have to have the faith that experiments on one sample are applicable to another.

The observation problem becomes more acute at the subatomic particle level. In 1927 Heisenberg noted that when observing the behaviour of small particles

> *The more precisely the position is determined, the less precisely the momentum is known in this instant, and vice versa . . . I believe that the existence of the classical "path" can be pregnantly formulated as follows: The "path" comes into existence only when we observe it.* [84]

Science provides an excellent methodology for understanding predictable behaviour, but it does not make claim to be able to provide all the answers that we need. There are unanswered and scientifically unanswerable questions that remain.

---

[83] http://imagine.gsfc.nasa.gov/docs/dict_ad.html#dark_matter accessed 23/2/13

[84] *Über den anschaulichen Inhalt der quantentheoretischen Kinematik und Mechanik* in Zeitschrift für Physik, 43 (1927) Further information about Heisenberg and the birth of quantum theory can be found at http://www.aip.org/history/heisenberg/p01.htm

God and Science in Conflict?

Supporters of Scientism often claim that there have been a number of fierce encounters where science has confronted Christianity, and given it a "bloody nose."[85] This claim is used as evidence that the hypothetical God is on the retreat and will eventually disappear.

Galileo is implied to have faced the Spanish Inquisition for challenging the Catholic Church about whether the sun moves round the earth or vice versa. Although Galileo was indeed tried before the Inquisition and sentenced to house arrest, it seems unlikely that this was due to the publication of the scientific theory. Galileo seems to have had quite a torrid relationship with the church, but worked with the blessing of the Pope, many cardinals and the Inquisition for many of his publications. For example it seems that he disagreed with transubstantiation, the Catholic dogma that bread and wine taken at communion in church actually becomes the body and blood of Jesus Christ.

> *A complaint against Galileo's Assayer (a treatise that Galileo published) is lodged by a person unknown to us. The complaint charges that the atomism espoused in the book cannot be squared with the official church doctrine regarding the Eucharist, in which bread and wine are "transubstantiated" into Christ's flesh and blood. After an investigation by the Inquisition, Galileo is cleared.*[86]

A more recent example of a supposed conflict between science and faith is the reporting of the 1860 Oxford evolution debate, often also known as the Huxley-Wilberforce Debate after two of the participants: Thomas Huxley and Bishop Samuel Wilberforce. Some

---

[85] *Slaying the Dragons – Destroying Mythis in the history of science and faith* Allan Chapman ISBN 976-0-7459-5583-4

[86] http://galileo.rice.edu/chron/galileo.html accessed 7th March 2012

> **Logical Fallacy: False dichotomy**
>
> If only two options are presented to a problem and then one is discounted by argument this implies that the other path must be followed. The fallacy lies in omitting other alternatives. For example, "You've either got to believe in God or Science, and since science is thoroughly researched and peer reviewed no intelligent person will fail to believe in it. Nobody with intelligence can believe in God."

claim that this was a fierce debate between science and the church, when evolution proved that there was no God.

However, it was more a discussion than a debate, and many scientists and philosophers participated. Wilberforce questioned certain specifics of Darwin's Theory of Evolution and Huxley was defending it, this was not a clash of church against science — there were churchmen, scientists and philosophers on all sides of the discussion. It seems that nobody considered the church was routed, and later all three major participants felt they had had the best of the discussion. Wilberforce wrote that, *"On Saturday Professor Henslow . . . called on me by name to address the Section on Darwin's theory. So I could not escape and had quite a long fight with Huxley. I think I thoroughly beat him."*[87] Huxley claimed *"[I was] the most popular man in Oxford for a full four & twenty hours afterwards."* Another biologist, Samuel Hooker clearly also thought that he had made the most important contribution and wrote that *"I have been congratulated and thanked by the blackest coats and whitest stocks in Oxford."*[88] Wilberforce and Darwin remained on good terms after the debate.

The Genesis Problem

---

[87] Samuel Wilberforce, letter to Sir Charles Anderson, July 3, 1860
[88] http://www.oum.ox.ac.uk/learning/htmls/debate.htm Accessed 1/4/13

Why do supporters of Scientism think that there is a conflict between science and religion? I suspect it is largely because at the start of the Bible we find the book of Genesis which begins with a description of God creating the world, plant, animals and man from nothing in six days. If this is read literally then it is clearly in conflict with science and evolution, but is that the correct way to interpret the book?

We don't really know where Genesis came from, but we do know it was written a very long time ago in human terms. It may even be the combination of two separate accounts. We know that the people who were writing it (where writing is used loosely as it was probably passed down by word of mouth) would not have understood any of the words in a modern day scientific description of the creation of the universe.

Unfortunately there seems to be an alliance between "New Atheists" and "Creationists" who both insist that the book of Genesis in the Bible must be read literally. I think it is clear that both misunderstand the purpose of the book. It was surely never written as a detailed scientific description of the creation process. More likely the passage was intended to convey that God created the world (universe) from nothing and that he sustains what he has created. That interpretation is completely consistent with what we have learnt from scientific discovery.

The problem for Creationists is that to interpret Genesis literally they must reject the Theory of Evolution, and so look ignorant in the eyes of the world. This is not a new issue however. In the early fifth century a minority of Christians also claimed that the account in Genesis was to be read literally. St Augustine was forthright in his criticism of such a position, writing:

> It is a disgraceful and dangerous thing for an infidel
> to hear a Christian, presumably giving the meaning
> of the Holy Scripture, talking nonsense on these
> topics; and we should take all means to prevent such
> an embarrassing situation . . . the shame is not so
> much that an ignorant individual is derided, but that

people outside the household of faith think our sacred writers held such opinions, and, to the great loss of those for whose salvation we toil, the writers of our Scriptures are criticised and rejected as unlearned men. [89]

One morning I felt the inspiration to write a more modern version of the Genesis account of creation, incorporating and alluding to the scientific discoveries of recent times. I hope that nobody chooses to take offence:

Before the beginning of time and matter in our universe, there was God. Of his works other than our universe we know nothing, but of his works in this universe we have learned much through the gift of our intellect. Of all his purpose in our universe we can know only what he has chosen to reveal to us, and he has revealed that we were his purpose. One purpose alone or one purpose among many is not for us to know.

God chose to create this universe. He created time, and then he tore nothingness into matter and antimatter, and in that great explosion from nothing he caused there to be an excess of matter over antimatter. And he causes matter to interact with matter through invisible forces acting across nothingness. And ripples of that rending apart of nothing remain until this day for us to observe with wonder.

Since God knows his plans, he chooses to cause matter to behave in a consistent way. He allows the tiniest particles to behave in individually unpredictable ways, but in community he causes them to follow his chosen laws. In the presence of

---

[89] *On the Literal Meaning of Genesis* Augustine, trans J.H.Taylor 1982

spirit, whether God's own or that of humans or other spiritual beings, God allows his laws to be suspended. God continues to sustain and guide his creation, acting as and when he chooses and allowing individuals to choose how to act.

And so for billions of years, although years were yet to be invented, the universe unrolled according to the laws that God had chosen. Particles formed into atoms, atoms formed into great stars and stars drew together into galaxies. The first stars grew to such a size that the interaction between the matter and the forces caused great energy and the explosion of the stars, and in those explosions new atoms were formed. God was making the building blocks of life, the carbon and the oxygen atoms. Out of those explosions, and according to God's laws of interaction new stars formed, and planets were formed around those stars.

One of those planets, the earth, had the right conditions for the next phase in God's plan. The planet was at first a molten mass, bombarded from space by asteroids and meteors as the turmoil of the formation of the particular sun and galaxy subsided. A crust was formed on the molten mass, and a gaseous atmosphere formed above the crust. In that atmosphere and on the crust, the carbon, hydrogen and oxygen atoms joined to form more complex short molecules. When the time was right, these short molecules formed into long chain molecules. These very special molecules continued to work according to the laws that God had chosen for the atoms and particles. The molecules had different purposes, some formed into cell membranes, some formed into little molecular machines, and some formed into very long instruction chains. And God caused them to be combined into what we today would call cells, and God had given them the mechanism to multiply in number.

To the first cells he gave the task of changing the atmosphere of the earth. Using the energy of the nearest star, the sun, the cells separated oxygen from carbon dioxide and pumped the oxygen into the atmosphere. For more than a billion years the cells carried out their task of preparing the atmosphere of the earth, getting ready for the more complex organisms that were next on his plan.

When conditions were right, the individual cells formed into groups or communities that were dependant on each other, where each cell in the group performed slightly different functions and so the new organism was able to both become larger but also to perform more complex functions. God gave the individual cells the means to evolve a mechanism that would carry the instructions for each cell in the group to perform its function, and to respond to the communications from other cells within the group. And so, multicellular organisms were formed.

The instructions embedded in each of these cells ran to billions of characters in length. The mechanisms of the cell and these instructions were both necessary for the cells to operate and grow, and to reproduce from generation to generation. God didn't plan to make all organisms identical, so he designed ways and means of bringing variation to the offspring of the organisms. He allowed "random" variations due to inaccurate copying, and he caused deliberate mixing of the instructions in one organism with another, requiring separate organisms to come together in order to create the next generation. The

130

organisms themselves thus had to live in partnership and community to survive.

So God had established a process of growing a wide diversity of organisms of increasing functionality that relied on each other to survive and thrive. Whilst each individual organism would be allowed to behave in an individual way, only those that were successful in progressing God's plan survived and reproduced. God chose to allow a process of competition to develop the organisms as he wanted; a process which required individual capability and cooperation between individual cells within an organism, and between organisms of the same type. Through this phase of God's plan he used the law of "survival of the fittest" to perfect each organism, and to select which organisms to perfect. The organisms didn't know anything of right and wrong.

But that was not the end of God's purpose, although it took billions of years to accomplish. His plans were greater than that, for there to be beings in his likeness; beings that would design and create, but more than that, beings that would know right from wrong, beings that would love, spiritual beings that would know and seek God himself.

So he selected one of the organisms and he planted his spirit in that organism and gave it an awareness of God himself, and he gave that organism the ability to know what is right and what is wrong, and he gave that organism the ability to choose to do what is right or what is wrong. That organism is mankind, the pinnacle of God's creation.

You might not be ready to accept this new account. Certainly it is still not literally correct, but maybe it is more relevant to today's society in the same way that the original Genesis was relevant to the society of its day. It conveys that all of us are spiritual and material beings, willed by God as the culmination of a creative process of unimaginable complexity spanning billions of years, following the creation of time itself. Mankind: created with the opportunity to know God and to relate to him, but allowed the alternative of rejecting and ignoring him.

Our Experience of Self

Science requires objective observation, and so must struggle to explain the subjective experience that (I assume) each person has of themselves. The only person who can know what it is to be me is me. It is impossible for anyone else to have the experience of being me, and so it is impossible to objectively measure the experience.

But we can add objective observation to subjective experience and speculate on questions such as: Where is our inventiveness, our thinking, our learning carried out? Where is our consciousness?

Is our experience of consciousness a function of our amazing brain, that giant organic computer in our skull? Perhaps it's the neurons reorganising the network pathways, establishing new connections; the brain constantly reprogramming itself. Perhaps it's the flow of electricity through the network of cells in our brain, through constantly opening and closing microscopic switches in our synapses.

The materialist worldview that matter is all the that there is, requires that there is nothing of consciousness, nothing of "us" that does not comprise the matter that makes up our brain; that our consciousness is an emergent property from the complex electrical interactions within our brain. But if this worldview is correct, what are the implications?

Computer Simulation

In his paper "Are you living in a computer simulation?"[90] Nick Bostrom explores the assumption that consciousness does indeed emerge as a result of the brain's complex construction and operation. Bostrom recognises that computer power is progressing at a massive rate and suggests that if we extrapolate the development then it will be possible to build computers with much greater calculating capability than we have in our human brains. He speculates that scientific knowledge will increase until it will be possible to simulate the operation of the brain, and that it will be possible to build a sufficiently complete model of the universe that it will be indistinguishable to the human mind from the real universe. Therefore, at some time in the future, man's descendants will be able to build a computer that will simulate the life of an individual human being, interacting with a simulated environment.

Further, it would be necessary and possible for that simulated human being to have other human beings to interact with in order that the simulation is complete. Since there will be a vast computational capacity and plenty of time then the computers would run a great many simulations. As he states in the introduction to his paper:

> . . . they could run a great many such simulations. Suppose that these simulated people are conscious (as they would be if the simulations were sufficiently fine-grained and if a certain quite widely accepted position in the philosophy of mind is correct). Then it could be the case that the vast majority of minds like ours do not belong to the original race but rather to people simulated by the advanced descendants of an original race.

---

[90] "Are you living in a computer simulation?" *Philosophical Quarterly* (2003) Vol. 53, No 211, pp.243-255. (First Version: 2001)) Nick Bostrom

Since we would be unable to recognise the difference between the real universe and the simulated universe, you and I cannot tell whether we are in a simulation or not. So on the basis there will be far more simulated minds than real ones, the statistical and logical conclusion is that we are all most likely to be simulations. I don't feel like a simulation, but the simulation would be so perfect that I couldn't know!

There are many assumptions that Bostrom has made, but they are assumptions that underpin much of Scientism and the materialist worldview. It seems ironic that the implication of the materialist worldview seems to be that we don't really exist in the material form that we think we do; our bodies are just a computer simulation.

There are perhaps 100 billion neurons in the brain, with around 1000 trillion connections between them. However, Stanford University have recently published work which suggests that the brain is orders of magnitude more complex than that. From their press release:

> (T)he brain's overall complexity is almost beyond belief, said Smith. "One synapse, by itself, is more like a microprocessor — with both memory-storage and information-processing elements — than a mere on/off switch. In fact, one synapse may contain on the order of 1,000 molecular-scale switches. A single human brain has more switches than all the computers and routers and Internet connections on earth.[91]

Maybe Bostrom's scenario is not quite so close. It may be that somehow this complexity crammed into such a small physical space leads to our experience of consciousness, but I don't find the idea convincing. Could a computer simulation of a brain appreciate beauty, could it feel love, could it really experience consciousness as we experience consciousness? Such extreme claims would demand extreme evidence.

---

[91]http://med.stanford.edu/ism/2010/november/neuron-imaging.html Accessed 1/4/13

After Death

A question that we all consider at some time is "what happens to us when we die?" If we exist simply within our material bodies then by implication our self dissipates, like the picture on the television screen when it is switched off. If we are more than our material bodies, then where do we go, what happens? Is there anyone who can tell us the answer?

There are people who have been pronounced dead, but who have then been revived and have described their experience. We might find out more from exploring what happens in near-death and out-of-body experiences.

Anecdotal evidence from family members of a dying loved one will often speak of there being a "calmness," a point at which the body appears to become just a body, when the person has left it. I have a friend who worked in a nursing home and is certain that she has seen something, like a blue light leaving the body at the point of death.

Neuroscientists can stimulate parts of the brain and cause our perception of where we are to move from being in our head to being somewhere outside of our bodies. If everything we perceive and experience is based on a processed model of the signals coming into the brain, and a disruption of those signals will change what we experience. Perhaps the out-of-body experience is simply moving our awareness of where we are to a different point in our perception model.

It is clear that out-of-body and near-death experiences actually happen; the number of reported cases is too high to doubt. One scientist who has been investigating these experiences is Dr Sam Parnia. He notes that although each near-death experience is different in detail, there are many very common experiences:

- Intense feelings of calmness.
- Travelling down a long dark tunnel.
- Being drawn into an intense loving light.

- Seeing your dead body from above.
- Meeting long-deceased relatives or friends.
- A few experience a brief form of "Hell" where they are drawn, petrified, into a dark swirling well of bitterness, hatred and fear.[92]

From his studies Dr Parnia has come to question many assumptions. For example, is there a single moment of death? It is possible to revive a clinically dead person; there are cases where a person can be resuscitated up to a few hours after death. So what has happened to the individual person during that time?

Ian McCormack was pronounced dead after being stung 5 times by box jellyfish.[93] He has described in detail his experience during the fifteen minutes that he was considered to be dead, and the profound positive change it made to his life. Many of those who survive death and have near-death experiences are transformed, living much more altruistic lives.

Dr Parnia compares death to what happens to stroke victims. In stroke victims a local part of the brain dies due to starvation of oxygen. In death the complete brain is starved of oxygen, and the cells stop functioning. Brain oxygen lasts perhaps 2 minutes, and the brain energy store lasts 4 minutes, after that the cells start to degrade. However, for a short period, perhaps up to a few hours, the cells are still "viable"; up until they have decayed the cell death may be reversible. Even if the precise definition of when we die is open to question, we can conclude that the cells in our bodies do indeed all die eventually, and that either our consciousness dies too, or goes somewhere else.

The brain is, and has to be, an incredibly complex entity. The task it has to carry out is immense; we can only begin to grasp the complexity and sophistication required. Our conscious mind has many facets: self-awareness, will, emotion, conscience, analytical

---

[92] http://vimeo.com/11302423 acccessed 8/7/13

[93] http://www.raised-from-the-dead.org.uk/accounts/m/mccormack-ian-s1-all.php accessed 4/3/13

capability. However it seems to me that there is still more to us than that: there is a "me," and I experience "Qualia."

Qualia

It is here that we move to the subjective, and it is difficult to see that scientific investigation can really proceed beyond speculation. But what are qualia? Here are two definitions:

> *Feelings and experiences vary widely. For example, I run my fingers over sandpaper, smell a skunk, feel a sharp pain in my finger, seem to see bright purple, become extremely angry. In each of these cases, I am the subject of a mental state with a very distinctive subjective character. There is something it is like for me to undergo each state, some phenomenology that it has. Philosophers often use the term "qualia" (singular "quale") to refer to the introspectively accessible, phenomenal aspects of our mental lives. In this standard, broad sense of the term, it is difficult to deny that there are qualia. Disagreement typically centres on which mental states have qualia, whether qualia are intrinsic qualities of their bearers, and how qualia relate to the physical world both inside and outside the head. The status of qualia is hotly debated in philosophy largely because it is central to a proper understanding of the nature of consciousness. Qualia are at the very heart of the mind-body problem.*[94]

and

> *Qualia . . . is a term used in philosophy to refer to individual instances of subjective, conscious experience. The term derives from a Latin word meaning for "what sort" or "what kind." Examples*

---

[94] Tye, Michael, *"Qualia,"* The Stanford Encyclopedia of Philosophy (Summer 2009 Edition), Edward N. Zalta (ed.), URL = <http://plato.stanford.edu/archives/sum2009/entries/qualia/>

of qualia are the pain of a headache, the taste of wine, the experience of taking a recreational drug, or the perceived redness of an evening sky. Daniel Dennett (b.1942), American philosopher and cognitive scientist, writes that qualia are "an unfamiliar term for something that could not be more familiar to each of us: the ways things seem to us." Erwin Schrödinger (1887-1961), the famous physicist, had this counter-materialist take: "The sensation of colour cannot be accounted for by the physicist's objective picture of light-waves. Could the physiologist account for it, if he had fuller knowledge than he has of the processes in the retina and the nervous processes set up by them in the optical nerve bundles and in the brain? I do not think so."

The importance of qualia in philosophy of mind comes largely from the fact that they are seen as posing a fundamental problem for materialist explanations of the mind-body problem. Much of the debate over their importance hinges on the definition of the term that is used, as various philosophers emphasise or deny the existence of certain features of qualia. As such, the nature and existence of qualia are controversial.[95]

The very question of what I am falls within this realm. What is the "I" that experiences these qualia? What does it mean to experience?

When I look at a picture, when I hear music, when I stab my finger with a pin, I am consciously experiencing something. But what is pain? Is it just an electrical impulse? How can I experience it? I don't experience the current flowing through the desk lamp next to me. What is the colour red? Is it a wavelength, or is it an interpretation of the wavelength? Can there be red without anyone

---

[95] http://en.wikipedia.org/wiki/Qualia accessed 4/3/13

to experience it? All of these things are referred to as qualia, and are inexplicable by science. They are so personal and experiential that we cannot investigate objectively. Yet they are amongst the most important things in the universe, at least for us as human beings. I don't find such things explicable from a purely materialist viewpoint, but I do find them consistent with the concept of each of us being something more, a self, what some refer to as a soul.

Sleep

It is easy to accept myself as a conscious individual when I am awake; I know that I am me, I am aware of my self. But when I am asleep is the real me the one in the dream, or is it the physical body that lies on the bed? At times I can be aware that I am dreaming; I learned as a child to stop myself when I was falling in my dreams. Does this mean that our self is in our dreams, even though our bodies are unconscious, dormant and physically recuperating?

Descartes

Rene Descartes in the 1600s made the famous comment "I think, therefore I am." He recognised that the only way we know we exist is by our thinking, our consciousness, our self-awareness. Descartes' statement was based on the fundamental fact that we experience our self. We don't know that anyone else or anything else exists, but we know that we exist. In essence, all that I actually know is that I think. I don't know that I have a body, I don't know that the keyboard I am typing on exists, or that you exist. All I know is that I think that they exist. But because I know I am thinking, I know that I exist even if my thoughts are all that there is. I think, therefore I exist. It is the root of any reality that we can experience. "We" are our only vantage point on the universe. It is our consciousness, not our physical body that is the true reality; the thing that actually makes us "us."

Descartes argued that since I can only be sure that I exist because I think, and not because I have a brain, then I don't need a brain for me to exist. He concluded that "self" and "brain" are separate and distinct things.

Plato

Going further back, Plato proposed that there is a material world and a world of "Forms" or ideas.

A form is an abstract property or quality. Take any property of an object; separate it from that object and consider it by itself, and you are contemplating a form. For example, if you separate the roundness of a basketball from its colour, its weight, etc. and consider just roundness by itself, you are thinking of the form of roundness. Plato held that this property existed apart from the basketball, in a different mode of existence than the basketball. The form is not just the idea of roundness you have in your mind. It exists independently of the basketball and independently of whether someone thinks of it. All round objects, not just this basketball, participate or copy this same form of roundness.[96]

Forms are eternal, non-material, pure, perfect, the ultimate reality and the cause of all things, and interconnected (the basketball is red and round). The "soul," or existence in the world of Forms, is united with the body until death when it will be separated and return to the world of Forms. True reality is that experience by the soul in the world of Forms.

Free Will

We all think we have free will; the ability to decide what to do or what not to do. We don't exercise free will in everything we do. Indeed, we are not aware of most of what we do but we are able to exercise our will when we choose to do so. Thinking itself is an example free will, we can choose where to take our thoughts—

---

[96]http://www.anselm.edu/homepage/dbanach/platform.htm accessed 4/3/13

although we don't always do so; it takes willpower to exercise free will.

However, if we are in a universe that operates according to fixed rules and laws (laws of physics) then it is extremely difficult to even imagine a mechanism for free will. Here is one attempt that I came across:

> We do make choices, in a sense. Our choices are determined by our brain state at the moment of choice, including the emotions we experience that motivate those choices. And that brain state is in turn the product of the interaction of our gene-environment wiring-up and all our previous experiences from conception through the instant before the choice. We don't even actually experience ourselves as having free will—we only think we experience our choices this way. [97]

On the same discussion thread was the comment:

> . . . given our understanding of determinism + undeterminism there is nothing left that explains exactly what free will could be, in the traditional sense. It's more a case of a challenge to those that assume free will to explain its mechanism.

In other words, the writer is saying that unless a physical mechanism for free will can be demonstrated then free will is an illusion. This is the logical fallacy "Appeal to Ignorance."

Would the computer characters in Bostrom's simulation have free will? [98] They could make choices, but only choices that result

---

[97] http://whyevolutionistrue.wordpress.com/2012/07/07/stephen-wolfram-and-i-on-free-will/#comment-237034 Posted July 7, 2012 at 7:13 am

[98] "Are you living in a computer simulation?" *Philosophical Quarterly* (2003) Vol. 53, No 211, pp.243-255. (First Version: 2001))

from the programming. The characters will not have free will—change the input to the simulation and the output will change.

Systems quickly become so complex that a minor change in an input parameter can cause the whole behaviour to appear unpredictable, like a gentle breath of wind causing a pin that is balanced on its point to fall in an apparently unpredictable direction. In the complex computer model it may <u>appear</u> that the characters have free will, but there is no mechanism for free will to operate. Bostrom's characters are computer simulations, and since we know that they are simulated by fixed equations it is easy to conclude that they do not have free will. If we believe that the world operates according to fixed equations then it also seems reasonable to conclude that we don't have free will.

Experience

But what is our practical experience? We live, we think, we evaluate—you are doing it now—we weigh up evidence. And then we decide to act. We might decide to scratch an itch, or not scratch an itch. But we might also leave our bodies to unconsciously deal with the itch, acting on autopilot without our consciously realising it. Nevertheless, we know that we can be aware, and that our thoughts can lead to action. Whilst there are trends in our actions, they cannot be predicted with certainty. Statistically we may respond in a fairly predictable way to a given set of stimulation, but it is not a certainty — we certainly feel that can choose to change how we respond. Are our choices really directed by a gentle breath of wind, like the balancing pin? It doesn't feel like it.

Subjective evidence says that we have free will, but objectively free will is a difficult (if not impossible) thing to test. Imagine I roll a coin down a ruler. I have no idea where it will come off, (how far down or which side it will fall off), so one could say that the ruler chooses where it will come off based on the balance of a number of factors—the initial direction of the penny, the orientation of the ruler with respect to gravity, the wind direction etc. That is the materialist view of free will.

However, imagine that there is someone holding the ruler who can choose to make a change in its orientation and so guide the coin to fall off the ruler at a given place. Deliberately choosing where the coin falls off is real free will, but the apparent choice made by an inanimate ruler is not. It is impossible to test whether the person holding the ruler deliberately chose where the coin will fall off.

Paradox

If we try to argue that we do not have free will then we tie ourselves in knots of paradox. If I claim that I don't have free will, am I not exercising free will in making that claim? Or if I am not exercising free will then the claim itself is just a string of words generated by a deterministic process and can have no meaning; it is only my free will that gives anything value or meaning.

Without free will I can have no opinion on free will itself because having an opinion means choosing what I think of it—but if our thought process is indeed only *"determined by our brain state at the moment of choice"* then that does not constitute an opinion, but only a determined response—I cannot <u>choose</u> what I think of it! Therefore, there is really also no me—the me that thinks it is having an opinion is deluded, but since delusion is a state of being drawn to <u>choose</u> a false conclusion I cannot be deluded because I cannot choose.

It seems to me far more useful to conclude that we do indeed have the free will that our experience tells us we have.

A mechanism?

Let's speculate and take up the *"challenge to those that assume free will to explain its mechanism."* How <u>might</u> free will be able to operate in a universe governed by a predictable and repeatable set of laws; the laws of physics?

I will emphasise that at this point I am speculating, but let's think back to quantum physics.

Any given particle shot at the two slits in the famous experiment will only make a mark in one place on the screen. The individual action of an individual particle is completely unpredictable, the laws of physics can only tell us that a large enough number behave in a predictable way.

It would be fully consistent with these observations if my "self," a non-physical entity were able to cause the behaviour of individual subatomic particles to respond to my will instead of responding according to blind chance. Like the hand holding the ruler that we rolled the coin down, "I" cause a given particle to hit the screen in a particular place. When I decide something, I influence the movement of a particular electron in a switch in a synapse in my brain and initiate a whole chain of very predictable events. I am not aware of how I do it, the mechanism is just something built into the body/soul interface.

I am not claiming that this is the mechanism, simply showing that there is potential for a mechanism to exist, commensurate with our understanding of physics. It is reasonable to expect a non-physical self, or soul, to be able to influence the material world.

So to sum up a little, by examining ourselves we may conclude (as Plato and Descartes concluded) that we are a non-physical self that interacts with our physical brain, triggering its incredibly complex machinery into action. Our self, which is additional to the observable material world, chooses the way that our material bodies in the material world will respond, thereby exercising our free will. And it is free will gives meaning to our life, our acts of kindness and love, our acts of goodness, and even acts of evil. Without free will there can be no good or evil, just actions. Without free will it means nothing to love or be loved. Without free will there is no morality; we cannot help what we do and so we cannot be accountable for what we do. Without free will nothing matters.

So I choose to have free will. And I conclude that I exercise my free will on the material world in a way that is consistent with the interface of a self with the laws of physics.

Experiences of God

It is clear that we can fully accept what science has discovered and still have reason to believe that God can influence things. The important question to each of us as individuals is "does he?"

Many people have had what they call "Spiritual Experiences," often described as encounters with God. A personal experience of this sort transforms a person's outlook from a position of intellectual questioning to a certain knowledge that God exists. This can be immensely frustrating for those pursuing the intellectual approach; "say what you like, I *know* that I had an encounter with Jesus Christ." Very unscientific! But very real.

Healing

There are many people who claim to have been miraculously healed following prayer: legs growing longer, pain disappearing, hearing restored and there are even reports of people being resurrected. Some reports are anecdotal; others have been more rigorously investigated.[99]

Some may be somatoform disorders (where the physical illness is caused solely by the mind) or psychosomatic disorders (where mental factors play a large role in the illness), and one can imagine that trusting that a healer will heal such a disorder will actually lead to healing. We know that the mind has incredible

---

[99] *The Miracles* H. Richard Casdorph ISBN 978-0882701721

potential to heal. Many people respond to hypnosis, perhaps giving up smoking or being able to lose weight, and there is an interesting example from the British Medical Journal of a boy being healed from a congenital recessive genetic disorder, following treatment by hypnosis.[100] [101] Such a disorder should not be responsive to hypnosis, and bizarrely, if the doctor had better understood the illness he would not have attempted treatment by hypnosis, and the child would not have been healed.

Another example is described by Dr Bruce Lipton[102]

> *My favourite example of scientific denial of the reality of mind-body interactions relates to an article that appeared in Science about nineteenth-century German physician, Robert Koch, who along with Pasteur founded the Germ Theory. The Germ Theory holds that bacteria and viruses are the primary cause of disease. A modified version of that theory is widely accepted now, but in Koch's day it was more controversial. One of Koch's critics was so convinced that the Germ Theory was wrong that he brazenly wolfed down a glass of water laced with vibrion choolerae, the bacterium Kick believed caused cholera. To everyone's astonishment, the man was completely unaffected by the virulent pathogen. The Science article published in 2000 describing the incident stated: "For unexplained reasons he remained symptom free, but nevertheless incorrect.*

---

[100] "A case of congenital ichthyosiform erythrodermia of Brocq treated by hypnosis" – AA Mason - *Br Med J.* 1952 Aug 23;2(4781):422-3
[101] http://www.ncbi.nlm.nih.gov/pmc/articles/PMC2021155/ accessed 16/6/13
[102] *The Biology of Belief* – Dr Bruce Lipton - ISBN 978-1-84850-335-9
Page 95

Lipton, clearly a little bitter with the scientific community, remarks that *"scientists blithely dismiss this and other embarrassing "messy" exceptions that spoil their theories."*

It is well known that placebos can be effective, and it has recently been reported that placebos can even be effective if we know that they are placebos.[103]

Faith Heals

It follows therefore that if one *believes* that there is a God that can heal, then he can heal. But what if one doesn't believe that God can heal, can he still heal? Consider the following passage from the Gospel of Matthew talking about Jesus:

> *He returned to Nazareth, his hometown. When he taught there in the synagogue, everyone was amazed and said, "Where does he get this wisdom and the power to do miracles?" Then they scoffed, "He's just the carpenter's son, and we know Mary, his mother, and his brothers — James, Joseph, Simon, and Judas. All his sisters live right here among us. Where did he learn all these things?" And they were deeply offended and refused to believe in him. Then Jesus told them, "A prophet is honoured everywhere except in his own hometown and among his own family."* **And so he did only a few miracles there because of their unbelief.** *(Matthew 13: 54-58)*

This might suggest that God cannot heal unless someone believes. An explanation might be that unbelief **blocks** such healing. In other words we can exercise or free will and choose to prevent God influencing our lives. However, there are examples of unbelieving

---

[103] Kaptchuk TJ, Friedlander E, Kelley JM, Sanchez MN, Kokkotou E, et al. (2010) "Placebos without Deception: A Randomized Controlled Trial in Irritable Bowel Syndrome". *PLoS ONE* 5(12): e15591. doi:10.1371/journal.pone.0015591

people who have been unconscious or even who have died, and have experienced healing.[104][105]

Discussion

It is clear that from earliest civilisation people have believed that there was some sort of God who was in charge of the world. Many of the oldest archaeological sites are thought to be places of worship, sacrifice or other appeasement of the God or Gods of early man. And for millennia philosophers have attempted to discern what God (if he exists) might be like and what his will is for us.

Yet today, there are some who look to a new god to explain everything: science. In the 2013 TV series *Wonders of Life—what is life?* Brian Cox said that:

> *"no matter how unscientific it sounds this, this idea that there is some kind of soul or spirit or animating force that makes us what we are that exists after our death is common . . . it feels right, it is hard to accept that you are . . . just something that emerges from an inanimate bag of stuff"*

We feel that we are more than just a machine, and yet we find a top scientist telling us to ignore that feeling and persuade ourselves that we are nothing more than collections of chemicals doing what they have to do according to physical laws. Do we have to agree with him? Clearly not; there is plenty of evidence to the contrary.

If we are immersed in the development or application of science we may have a problem with the idea of God. Scientific language and method do not allow the scientist to resort to miracles in order to explain the universe. Science is about finding laws that match and predict the behaviour of the universe. However, the laws

---

[104]http://www.cbn.com/700club/features/amazing/Duane_Andrews_043010.aspx accessed 4/3/13

[105]http://www.cbn.com/700club/features/amazing/Jeff-Markin-Chauncey-Crandall-091510.aspx accessed 4/3/13

are simply equations which appear to describe the behaviour of the universe. The reality is the universe, not the equations.

If we can see that every time we drop an apple it falls to the ground with a law-like predictability, then we might struggle to see how a God could actually influence anything; matter follows laws, so how could God intervene, the laws would not allow it? Even if God did make everything, if he did create the material universe, then once he's set up the physical laws and created the matter how can he take any further part? And if he can't influence things then some would argue, what is the point of even thinking about the issue—he's set everything rolling and taken a vacation. Or is he a God who created the Big Bang and continues to sustain the universe through the laws of physics?

Science takes as read that the universe had the ability to come into existence and continue to exist. Science cannot comment on why that is the case. When we watch gravity at work, or a cell in action it can become so familiar that we might cease to question why it should be so.

> **Logical Fallacy: Begging the question**
>
> Often an argument can be presented that the listener finds that he is comfortable to accept, but with deeper examination he discovers that there is actually no evidence on which to base that acceptance. The argument evades the real question.

Our experiments have found that much of the behaviour of the universe is predictable, but it is an act of faith to assume that it is <u>all</u> predictable <u>all</u> of the time. Such an act of faith cannot allow belief in miracles.

A man walking on water is a miracle—it is not a repeatable event. Since it is not a repeatable event it cannot be predicted or tested by scientific methods. Miracles fall outside of the realm of science but that does not mean that they cannot happen. We will all know that Jesus is said to have performed miracles. The descriptions of the miracles are well documented. Why should we doubt that they happened, unless we have complete faith in our common sense view that they just don't happen? Yet we have seen that the universe takes little heed of common sense.

Perhaps, if we were to believe that miracles can happen we might start to see more of them? If we look for them, maybe we will find them, like in quantum physics; look for a particle and you find a particle, look for a wave and you find a wave? Perhaps what we can experience and achieve is simply limited by our belief, our faith and our worldview?

How do we feel about the following; do we believe it?

> *Through the eyes of a TV documentary crew I have watched a little old Tai Chi master hold at bay a handful of healthy young men trying to budge him from his standing position. With ever so slight a shrug he gathered all the energy — Chi — they threw at him and reflected it back, sending them all sprawling. One of the sprawled commented he might as well have been trying to topple a brick wall and that the force that toppled him was like a shock wave.*
>
> . . .
>
> *I have seen also a man crouch over a crumpled ball of paper. Holding his hands above the ball he grimaced slightly. The paper burst in flames. When a member of the video crew expressed some doubt, the man had the crewmember lie down. This time the hands unleashed into the other's abdomen what the crewmember described as "a large jolt of electricity."*
> 106

If we can accept that such things can happen as a result of the human mind, then it is completely rational to consider that there might be a God who can and does influence things. We demonstrate

---

106 http://www.synaptic.bc.ca/ejournal/thedark.htm#HEISENBERG accessed 11/3/13

that our mind or soul influences things every day, why can't we expect a God to do the same? If we accept this as a possibility then our outlook has to change.

There are many things that we haven't experienced that we accept might happen. Perhaps the story above about the Tai Chi master might have changed how we feel. If we accept that things happen that are outside of the realm of science then we can allow that God can be intimately involved in the formation and development of the universe, sustaining the evolutionary process, and the daily operation of our bodies.

We have seen indications, such as convergent evolution, that God created and maintains the universe in such a way that the outcome is inevitable, although the precise route was not pre-determined. Individual free will is possible within the overall purpose. When we walk to work, we don't design the route we will take, step by step. We decide the outcome (get to work) and we have the means to get there (our legs) but our journey is unpredictable.

But if this is the case, then why would God have any need for miracles? Miracles are not God's occasional supernatural tinkering with the evolution of the universe; they have a very different purpose. They are often personal experiences, bringing good to the recipients. And Jesus' miracles were intended to grab the attention. Would anyone have taken particular notice of him if he had not performed miracles, or if he had not been raised to life after his crucifixion? Of course not! He had a message to deliver, and he used miracles to make people listen.

However, if a miracle were to become commonplace it would no longer be a miracle; it would be amenable to the repeatability test of science. And then we might conclude that we could understand it because it is repeatable. We are immersed in the most amazing world, and yet it is so familiar that we don't consider it a miracle.

The world's scientists are working hard to uncover the secrets of the universe. But the outcome can never be to conclude that there is no God. Such a conclusion would ignore the evidence that stares us in the face every moment of every day. The continued existence and consistent behaviour of the universe points to a sustaining essence or force. Scientists give the name "Laws of Physics" to the power that sustains the universe. In the past people gave the name "God." The two are clearly the same; God is what we now also call the Laws of Physics.

Scientific discoveries can be relied on to sufficient degree to make a good estimate of the age of the earth, and the phases in its construction that it must have gone through; the coagulation into a molten mass, the cooling and formation of a crust, the separation of land and water, the initiation of life in the form of small bacteria that then over hundreds of millions of years cleaned and oxygenated the atmosphere, the development of more and more complex life-forms, the development of self-awareness and intelligence, and the development of machines and technology.

The process reminds us of the process that we go through when we make anything. We purposely dig iron ore out of the ground, refine it in furnaces, manipulate it in machines, join complex parts together and produce cars, washing machines and fridges.

The progression of the universe from the Big Bang to the present day suggests a purpose behind the universe. Some might call that purpose "blind chance" but if so it is blind chance operating under the dominion of the laws of physics / the will of God. Whatever the semantics, it appears that God sustains the universe for a purpose.

Chapter 5: Reason Leads to a Sound Definition of God

In our day-to-day life, the things that actually matter to each of us remain as they have always been. We sit in our gardens enjoying the warmth of the sunshine on our faces, a glass of wine or beer in our hands, and the company of friends around us. Even the most ardent materialist will, when off duty, enjoy a good film, concert or meal, feel the joy of the sunny mountaintop, feel angered by injustice, and know the need to feel loved. Whilst science can enhance aspects of life we need to find peace of mind, wellness of being, love, and purpose.

The view of Scientism is that love, honour, joy, virtue, morality, in fact any aspects of life that really matter to us, are "emergent properties." To my mind that is shorthand for saying "we don't know what they are," and it belittles their value.

Using the term "emergent" in this way expresses the opinion that none of these things existed before man expressed them. I disagree with that opinion. If I free myself from the materialist dogma of Scientism, reason tells me that love has always existed. Our experience of love is an expression of the essence of love. A rose was beautiful before we gave beauty a name.

Reason

Anselm

In the 11th century, Anselm of Canterbury (the then archbishop) explored what God might be like in his essay Monologion[107]. At that time people were not constrained by the materialist dogma. Anselm was happy to explore the non-material things: love, justice, purpose, hope.

---

[107] *Anselm of Canterbury: The Major Works* (Oxford World's Classics) ISBN 978-0199540082

Anselm identifies that an act of love is carried out through Love, and an act of justice is carried out through Justice. If Love did not exist then one could not carry out an act of love.

And it is also through Goodness that we are able to carry out an act of love, or of justice, or . . . . Love, Justice, Joy exist through and are therefore lesser than Goodness. Goodness is the ultimate "non-material" thing or essence, and it exists through itself.

An analogy might be that something red is red through Redness, and that it is also red through Colour. We can see that some things are more-red than others. In a similar manner we can also perceive that some acts are express more love than others; there can be great love, or great justice, or great goodness. We can imagine that for any great goodness there could be a goodness that is just a little greater . . . until we reach infinite goodness. And so everything that is good in any way is less than, or within that infinite or Supreme Goodness.

Everything exists through something and everything non-material exists through Supreme Goodness. But everything must exist through one thing. If we imagine that there were more than one thing, then either there would be one thing through which each of the "more than one thing" was able to exist—which would itself then be the one thing, or the two things might both exist through a "power to exist through oneself"—which would then be the one thing, or they would exist mutually through each other—which Anselm says defies reason.

. . . Brought Up to Date

Let's extend that thinking to the modern day. It is clear that either nothing caused the Big Bang, or something caused it. If "nothing caused it" then it happened because it could happen. Yet the ability to happen is not "nothing," it is "the ability to happen" so that doesn't work. At minimum there had to be "the ability for the Big Bang to happen."

So it seems to me that we must to conclude that something caused the Big Bang. Something had the ability to cause the universe to exist and to cause it to operate in a particular way; something that is not this universe, but a creator, or creative essence.

If Something set the universe running, why does it continue to run? Is it simply because it can? Is it because there are laws that ensure that it does? If so, we must conclude that something must be ensuring that the laws are maintained. In any case, Something must be sustaining the existence of the universe, the same Something that brought the universe into existence in the first place (it defies reason to consider one Something handing over the universe to another Something once it's up and running.)

To explain the beginning and continuation of the universe there needs to be a Something, which was not caused by anything else, that has simply always been; being outside of time (which only began at the Big Bang) that Something is eternal.

So the universe exists, and it exists through Something. As described above, non-material things exist through Supreme Goodness. Therefore, since everything can only exist through one thing, either the universe exists through Supreme Goodness, or Supreme Goodness exists through the universe. But can Supreme Goodness exist through the universe? We can conceive that there are other universes, but it is inconceivable that those other universes exist without Supreme Goodness; since it is non-material, Supreme Goodness cannot be constrained within a material context. Therefore it is impossible that Supreme Goodness exists through the universe. The universe must exist through Supreme Goodness. There can only be one Supreme Goodness—which we can call God.

So reason tells us that God is a non-material, eternal creative essence that also sustains the universe.

Good and Evil

It is clear that human beings are not only able to investigate and understand the normal behaviour of matter, but are also capable of understanding the difference between right and wrong, good and evil. We can choose to do things which we know we ought not to do.

We experience internal conflict and temptation to do what we know is wrong for some short term gratification.

Whilst the details of morality may differ according to different opinion or culture, we all know that there is a good or an evil direction, and most of us want to choose to be "good." This is the essence of Goodness that Anselm talked of, and we are aware of course of an essence that is evil. This essence is not something that you can touch; it is not a material thing. But neither can you touch the laws of physics. We can give these powers separate names: the laws of physics, the essence of Goodness, or a single name: God.

Self

Individual responsibility and operation of society is based on our free-will to decide how to behave; whether to be good or evil. Yet moral decision-making and self-awareness both lie outside of the predictable behaviour of matter. Both are evidence for a self; an essence of "us" which doesn't lie in the observable material world.

It is irrational to conclude that we would have this knowledge and free will but that a purposeful creator would not. It is not reasonable to imagine that we have developed attributes that are greater than the creator / creative essence. Therefore we can conclude that the purposeful creator of the universe also has an essence of Self. So God is more than the laws of physics and the essence of Goodness. We can conclude that God must be some form of individual. Indeed, there are many people who maintain that they have had a personal experience of God.

Material and Spirit

Neuroscientist Michael Graziano has speculated on the connection between the material and the spirit world. His book *God Soul Mind Brain* has the stated aim to describe *"the mechanistic understanding of the spirit world."* With this background he makes the assumption that the mechanism is the reality and perception is the illusion.

. . . we do not perceive the world as it is, the brain constructs a simulated world.

. . . colour is not actually out there. . . . The same set of wavelengths may look green to you in a different context or grey or blue

. . . We experience the model rather than the reality
[108]

The statements are fascinating reminders of what the brain does: it constructs a simulated world, it provides the stimulus to allow the experience of colours, and it somehow appears to create a model of the world in our brains.

However, it is an unjustified assertion that the mechanism is the reality and the perception is the illusion. It is like saying that the material pages of a book and the printed ink are the reality, and the story that the book tells or the information that it contains is not the reality. Whilst nobody would disagree that the book is the material and the story is not, which of them is the reality; which is the real book?

In a book, we read the words rather than perceiving the paper and letters and we construct in our imagination a picture and an experience based on the words and story within the book. In terms of the value to a human being, the book is the words, not the paper and ink. War and Peace is a famous story, the paper that it was written on was just the framework for holding it. The story is eternal although the paper decays. To a human being, only the story is important.

Consider a work of art; the material is not the masterpiece, it is merely a framework which holds the masterpiece. The canvas and paint is meaningless, the picture is the meaning.

When individuals experience God (spiritual experience) then of course this is associated with the circuitry in the brain, in the same

[108] Michael S. A. Graziano: *God Soul Mind Brain: A Neuroscientist's Reflections on the Spirit World* ISBN 978-1935248118

way that War and Peace is associated with paper and ink. But we cannot dismiss it as not being a true experience of God.

The material universe is meaningless until it is perceived, the perception of it gives it meaning, and maybe even the substance. When we look at the quantum level of the material, there is no such thing as paper or ink. There are particles and forces that we cannot understand; yet they are only potentialities until they are observed. What we consider material reality only becomes real and performs its function when it is perceived and observed.

It is the non-material that motivates us, the non-material that leads to progress. The non-material is master over matter. The non-material is the meaning.

The butterfly nebula is beautiful when it is observed; without observation it is meaningless.

Two "bags of stuff" are meaningless, but the intimate relationship between two people who are in love has immense meaning and purpose.

If we can free ourselves of the dogma of materialism then we can understand that the physical universe is just the canvas on which to paint the meaning.

God Within Us

As Anselm wrote, everything is what it is through supreme goodness, through God, so we are what we are through and within God. Jesus spoke of God living in us and us in him, and we are told that God is love, and that we are made in his image. Jesus said that "if you have seen me, you have seen the father." He wasn't talking about his flesh, but his character, his behaviour, his "spirit." Our framework (our body and brain) is a small part of a material universe that is created and sustained by God. If that universe is within God, part of God, then we too are "in him," as he is "in us."

Who would disagree that there is a "spirit of Christmas," all of society embracing a season of joy and giving? People speak of the true spirit of Christmas; we know that there is something that transcends each of us as individuals. It is part of the sprit that is God.

When we observe a beautiful woodland track, sunlight shining through the leaves to create a dappled light settling on a trickling stream, that beauty is part of the essence that is God.

When we listen to a sublime piece of music that moves us to tears, or an energising rock ballad that lifts our hearts with passion, we are experiencing part of God.

When we love someone, our love is part of the supreme love that is God.

When we meet friends in a party, in a community, that spirit of community is part of God's spirit of community.

If we can accept that the greater reality is the spirit, and the material is just the framework then we can see God and the universe in a whole new light. The universe is the canvas for a cosmic work of art, a magnificent symphony of action and beauty. Our bodies are a molecular dance of astonishing intricacy.

Of all creatures, we are permitted to explore and understand through science. We are permitted to glimpse the canvas and participate in the dance; characters created by the dance. Characters emerging as individual caring, loving, interacting beings partaking of some of the glory that is the story; individual masterpieces beyond the beautiful, whose reality is our character, our choices, our nature, our soul.

We are creatures of purpose and with purpose. Creatures honoured with the possibility of relating to our creator: the master artist, engineer, scientist, musician, teacher, parent, and friend. But never are we his equal.

But if we are simply very short lived transient accidents in one of many universes then so many things become meaningless, with no eternal value. Poems, works of art, the Holocaust, films, music, love, all will all be swept away when the sun explodes and we are as meaningful as a rock tumbling down a hillside.

So I come back to my one permitted preconception: that we matter. If we matter, then evidence and reason tells me that there is a God, and tells me a lot about what he is like.

Some Challenges

Suffering and an Omnipotent God

It is argued that there is far too much suffering in the world for there to be an all-powerful, all-knowing, all loving God. Suffering, it is argued, would be understandable if God had only two of the characteristics; if he's all-powerful and all-knowing but he isn't all loving, seems to work for instance. Assuming that we accept the scientific timescales and description of evolution, then for millions of years different animals have torn each other to pieces. Indeed, the whole process of natural selection appears to be based on brutality and suffering—kill off the weak, only the strong survive. Natural selection does not seem to be a very moral method for an all-powerful God to use to achieve his ends.

Our distaste of the idea stems from a number of things. One is that we are able to empathise, to imagine ourselves in the position of the suffering animal. We imagine that we would not like being torn to pieces, and we assume that neither does the animal. But underlying this is the assumption that the animal has the same cognitive abilities and the same feelings and "me-ness" that we do. I'm not saying that animals do or don't, but pointing out that it's an assumption that we make.

> **Logical fallacy: Contrary hypothesis**
>
> This is where a hypothesis or statement is cannot be consistent with itself. A common example of this is "If God is omnipotent, can he make a weight that is too heavy for him to lift?" and another is "All truth is relative."

We assume that the event is indeed painful. I recall reading the account of a man who had set fire to himself in an attempted suicide, and that he described that it was not particularly painful at the time. I recently had an accident where I cut my lip and needed 8 stitches. I noted at the time that it was not particularly painful, but those looking on were very distressed.

Suffering depends on our response to it. Someone with a "victim" outlook will view a small pain as suffering, but others will willingly endure much more pain to achieve a beneficial outcome — just look at how people choose to "suffer" childbirth, or dental treatment (before injections anyway), or cosmetic surgery, or rigorous athletic training. These examples lead us to recognise that it is an assumption that suffering is a bad thing. Remember too that suffering is transient; there is always hope for the future.

Nevertheless, we feel that an omnipotent God should be able to find an alternative way to achieve the same end; that God could have made the universe and life in a way that didn't require suffering. Perhaps that's why some Christians remain attached to the idea of God creating everything in six days, and that there was no death and suffering until Adam and Eve ate the apple in the Garden of Eden in disobedience to a direct order from God. But that doesn't really work either; God could simply not have planted that particular apple tree.

But imagine that it was possible to create a universe with no suffering, would there be any way of creating such a universe that didn't cause every living thing to be a robot? Nobody would be able to do anything wrong because wrong deeds are a cause of suffering. We wouldn't be able to choose whether to be nice or nasty — because if we and everyone else were allowed to choose then there would be suffering. There could be no free will. There could be no honour or dignity, no bravery. We would just be mindless machines, God's puppets.

So it is reasonable to conclude that an all-powerful, all-knowing, all loving God decided to create the universe with suffering, in order to achieve something grander. And if we believe what we read about Jesus then we know that God partook of suffering, so He did not subject us to "do as I say, not as I do." When we suffer, we know that God has been there too and is still there alongside us.

When we are suffering, we need strength and encouragement and we can get both of them from knowing that we are within God's will and love. What consolation would it be to conclude that because we are suffering, it shows that God doesn't exist or that if he does exist, he doesn't love us? That road leads to despair and bitterness.

The existence of suffering is not relevant in seeking a rational proof for or against God, although it has been influential in the faith choices of individuals.

Heaven and Hell

A common view of Heaven is that it is a reward for being good. Be good in this life and then you can go and "have a ball" in Heaven—no longer having the restraint of having to pass the entrance exam. Indeed, some believe that when a martyr gets to Heaven he is immediately met by seventy-two virgins and promised everlasting happiness.

Maybe our parents said things like "be nice or you won't go to Heaven," in the same way that they might have said "Do your homework or you won't go to university." Perhaps we grew up thinking that the final test will be to weigh our good deeds against our bad deeds, and if the scales tip the right way we get to Heaven.

Then there is Pascal's wager. Put simply, if you believe in God and he exists then you get to Heaven, if you believe and he doesn't you simply cease to exist when you die—no negative consequences, so a safe thing to do. If you don't believe in God and he doesn't exist then you simply cease to exist when you die, but if you are wrong you suffer in Hell—a serious negative consequence, not a safe thing to do. A friend likes to turn Pascal's wager upside down and says something like, "If I don't believe in God and find out Heaven is real then I get a double bonus as I haven't had to do all the religious stuff and I get to Heaven as well."

But is Heaven like any of these concepts? Let's apply some reason to the question.

I don't invite people to my house as a reward for them being good. I invite them because I like them.

I don't feel I have a right to go to someone else's house because I've been good. I only go because I want to get to know them better and expect to like them.

If Heaven is God's house, wouldn't we expect a similar situation to apply? Isn't it a cheek to expect to go to his house just because we've done good deeds? Isn't it reasonable to only go if we want to get to meet God? Would we expect to treat God with less respect than we would treat our neighbours?

And what of this idea that once we get there we can just enjoy all the things we've given up to get there? Seventy-two virgins . . . I wonder if they would consider it Heaven.

And that's really the point. Heaven is not set up for me as an individual to live in wanton pleasure to the detriment of everyone else. Heaven must be a place where everyone lives for the good of everyone else—otherwise it wouldn't be Heaven. A chaplain I know would say "Sin can't get into Heaven." If sin was allowed, Heaven would be the same as here; it would not be Heaven.

If you or I want to hold on to our selfish ways, if we want to hold on to any of our "sin" then we cannot be allowed to enter. We need a transforming of our mind to be able to enjoy Heaven; Heaven would be "Hell" if we didn't enjoy and thrive on being selfless and loving.

The issue is not "be good and go to Heaven." We need to be willing to undergo complete renewal of our way of thinking if we want to be fitted for Heaven; we need a pure "heart." That's what so much of Christ's teaching was all about—how to be completely selfless and loving, putting others before oneself, preparing ourselves for Heaven.

But if there is a Heaven, is there also a Hell?

Nobody really knows if Hell is real, if anyone will go there, or if it is eternal suffering. But we do know that the prospect of eternal painful punishment for simply not being able to believe in God does seem rather an extreme punishment and doesn't seem consistent with what Christians claim to be an infinitely loving and faithful God.

It is sad when discussions between ardent Evangelical Christians and New Atheists end up with a comment like: "Well you're wrong, and you're going to find out when you get to Hell." It seems perverse to develop a theology that insists that those who don't "pray the sinners prayer" (a relatively recent invention) are not "saved" and will go to Hell, particularly if there are alternative interpretations of the Bible which are far more consistent with a loving God.

Yes Jesus refers to Hell, for example:

> And if your hand—even your stronger hand — causes you to sin, cut it off and throw it away. It is better for you to lose one part of your body than for your whole body to be thrown into Hell. Matthew 5:30

And

> But I say, if you are even angry with someone, you are subject to judgement! If you call someone an idiot, you are in danger of being brought before the court. And if you curse someone, you are in danger of the fires of Hell. Matthew 5:22

But it seems to me that it is extrapolating a long way to reach the Evangelical position. Clearly the concept of Hell emphasises the importance of what he is saying, but it could easily be taken as a literary device for that purpose alone. In a trivial way we might say "that was better than a poke in the eye."

In one of St Paul's letters he describes that

I am convinced that nothing can ever separate us from God's love. Neither death nor life, neither angels nor demons, neither our fears for today nor our worries about tomorrow—not even the powers of Hell can separate us from God's love. Romans 8:38

That seems far more consistent with the character of God; that his love is so great that he wouldn't even let something as horrific as the concept of Hell get between us.

A Sound Definition of God

When we pull together all the pointers outlined above, we can develop a view of what God might be like. This is incredibly important. A false view of God will lead to misunderstanding and conflict, and will obscure the truth about our purpose.

My first conclusion is that there is more than just the material universe, more than the "stuff" that Brian Cox referred to. In order to develop our understanding of God we must include everything, not just "stuff." And I conclude that if we consider all the available evidence (everything) then that evidence points to God.

So for me this is the God of science and reason. A God who was there before the universe began:

- An un-created, creator God who gave "nothing" the ability to become "something."
- A God who sustains the very fabric of the universe. A God who actually is the laws of physics, who benevolently sustains providence to bring life out of a set of chemicals.
- A God who imbues the chemical dance that is us with the ability to feel, to taste, to see, to experience: love, joy, peace, fulfilment, intellectual challenge, selflessness, forgiveness, anger, hate, disgust, bitterness.
- A God who is love, joy, peace, fulfilment, supreme goodness.
- A God who allows us to experience both the good and the bad, and allows us to choose which path to follow.

- A God who chooses to be intimately involved with the universe and in particular with us, the human race.

In short, a God of <u>everything</u>.

Chapter 6: Jesus Lived and Spoke for God

Science and reason have pointed to a God of everything, but we still know little of him. There are still things which elude our grasp. There are things about me that you will only know if I reveal them to you. Many people have claimed to have received just such revelations from God. In recent years President Bush claimed "God told me to invade Iraq."[109] Unfortunately, people being people, some have claimed to know God's will and sought to impose it on others through less than pleasant means. Maybe some make the claim honestly; others may make the claim to justify their decisions.

Decent people, wanting to be good and wanting to find purpose and wholeness, might be put off exploring God and religion by some of the ills that have been apparently been done in his name.

Opponents of religion often quote that without it there would have been no Crusades, no Spanish Inquisition, no "Northern Ireland" problem, no Hindu/Moslem violence in India. Even today there are some who claim to be Christians, yet who preach with venom and hatred. The Westboro Baptist Church "God Hates Fags" campaign is one example.

If God doesn't exist then perhaps religion has served its purpose and should indeed be disbanded. Yet we have deduced that there seems to be a God, a creating and sustaining essence of goodness. Is he really a fag-hating God? Does religion really represent him?

Maybe the problem lies with human nature; men wanting to control and manipulate others. In some cases religion has become indistinguishable from politics or tribalism. Maybe many of those who claim to speak for God are simply wrong; the Westborough Baptists certainly don't seem to have understood Christ's teaching.

---

[109]http://www.bbc.co.uk/pressoffice/pressreleases/stories/2005/10_october/06/bush.shtml accessed 9/6/13

There have been plenty of atrocities carried out that are NOT in the name of religion: elimination of millions of people in the Congo under the orders of King Leopold II, suppression and mass murdering of the Russian people under Stalin, mass extermination and suppression of democracy under Hitler, suppression and mass murdering of the Chinese people under Mao and the communist regime, the Tiananmen Square massacre, genocide in Rwanda.

The Holocaust was a terrible thing, and many Jews lost their faith in God as a result. How could God allow such suffering? Chief Rabbi Jonathan Sacks tells that he too lost faith as a result of the Holocaust, but he lost his faith in mankind.[110] Yes, individual men and women can and do perform acts of great bravery, self-sacrifice and love, but some also do terrible deeds. In a mob, evil so readily prevails. An individual may not go and lynch his neighbour, but as part of a crowd he may well burn his house and kill his family too.

Historicity of Jesus Christ

There is one religion whose founder claimed that "if you have seen me you have seen God," who referred to God as his father, and claimed that he lived in the father, and the father lived in him. If that was true, then he could certainly tell us what God's will is. And if people believed him then he could amass immense power. Yet he did not make his claims in order to secure his position. Quite the opposite, he taught that the least would be the greatest and the first would be last. He allowed himself to be brutally killed by his enemies, even preventing his followers from coming to his defence. His name is Jesus.

Whilst others who have founded religions have claimed to have written what God told them to write, Jesus claimed that God was within him—no middle man, no interpretation—he was

---

[110] *The Case for God* BBC1 6th Sept 2010 The Chief Rabbi Lord Jonathan Sacks discussion with Professor Lisa Jardine

speaking as God. If that is true then the implications are profound, and it's really important to find out what he actually said.

It is clear that many at the time were convinced that he spoke the truth, and if we conclude that they are correct then it's important to know whether the records of what he said are historically accurate. We don't want to be misled by later interpretations or additions; we want the original documents. We need to know the historical reliability of the accounts of his life and works in the New Testament; when was it written, by whom, and how we can judge if it is an accurate description. We need to look at the biblical documents themselves, but also other early documents, including apocryphal gospels that are not included in the Bible.

Even a sound historical provenance of the documents does not conclusively prove that the events described therein happened. It is strong evidence since, as we will see, the documents were written within the lifespan of eye witnesses to what happened, and if the documents contained lies then it is unlikely that they would have survived uncorrected. Nevertheless, a determined sceptic can hold to the opinion that they were written with an agenda.

However, we must remember the context in which they were written. The followers of Jesus were convinced that he was the promised Messiah. They were not all simple people who were easily deluded, many were highly intelligent, and many were strict Jews or leaders in the Jewish community. All risked violent death by following Jesus.

Transpose things to the present day, and ask what would convince someone in (say) the Catholic Church that I was the Messiah. I wouldn't be very successful if all I did was walk in to a church an offer some good moral teaching. There have been thousands of excellent moral teachers, but that's no reason to suppose that they are the Messiah. There must have been something very profound that caused people to choose to believe Jesus and follow him to their own death. And something very profound is described in the historical accounts. So, we should not read the accounts to conclude that profound things happened, but we realise that profound things must have happened and we read the accounts to find out what they were. It's an important difference.

The New Testament Documents

Much of the historical evidence of what Jesus said and did comes from the four Gospel accounts in the New Testament. The word "gospel" comes from old English "god"(good) and "spell" (news), hence "gospel" literally means "good news." The New Testament also includes the Book of Acts, various letters from members of the early church, and the book of Revelation. The gospels are accounts of the life, death and resurrection of Jesus. The Book of Acts records the events immediately after the crucifixion and resurrection of Jesus. The letters, from Paul, from the disciples Peter and John, and James the brother of Jesus are mainly giving advice and interpreting Jesus' life and death in practical and spiritual terms. The New Testament ends with the book of Revelation; an apocalyptic document describing a vision or "revelation" that author experienced.

Some very old fragments of New Testament documents survive today, although the passage of time means that none of the original Gospel documents are preserved. However, the practice of copying and translating the documents ensures that the content is accurately preserved. There are many fragments of manuscripts from the second and third centuries, and the earliest full manuscript of the gospels dates from the early third century.[111]

There have been many generations of copying, with each copy introducing the possibility of copying mistakes. There is clear evidence that this happened, for instance some copies include repeated phrases. However, comparing the many copies of the New Testament documents allows us to be confident of the original text. Where there are discrepancies between manuscripts a number of

---

[111] "Evidence of Manuscripts" Dr. Dirk Jongkind. *The Authentic Gospels: New Evidence*, St Helen's Bishopsgate, London, June 2010

tests can be used to determine the original text. Tests include the number of manuscripts with each version, the age of the manuscripts, the quality (number of discrepancies / errors) of each manuscript, the geographical spread of the manuscript, the difficulty in reading the text (scribes may try to make the text easier), and the type of language.

Tracking the errors in the copying process can be used in a similar way to using errors in the DNA replication process to determine the "parentage" of given copy. However, errors can be eliminated in subsequent copies if a scribe notices and corrects the mistake in the document that he is copying.

Dates

How do scholars determine exactly when the originals of the documents were written? Various techniques are used, including references to key events for which dates are known from other sources (such as destruction of Jerusalem in AD 70), and from references made in other letters or documents for which dates may be better known. Researchers will learn early languages, the development of calligraphic styles, the sources and types of materials used for writing. They will examine first hand at original manuscripts and can even determine that a group of scribes worked on particular documents, and which parts were written by the same scribe[112].

It is generally agreed that all of the documents were complete in their present form by AD 100, seventy years after the crucifixion. The earliest of the four gospels is thought to be Mark, around AD 65, with Matthew and Luke being between 5 and 20 years later. The Gospel of John is thought to be the latest of the four gospels dating around AD 90-100.

The Gospel of Luke and the Book of Acts are both addressed to a "most honourable Theophilus," with Acts beginning "In my first

---

[112] "Evidence of Manuscripts" Dr. Dirk Jongkind. *The Authentic Gospels: New Evidence*, St Helen's Bishopsgate, London, June 2010

book I told you, Theophilus . . . ." So Acts is naturally believed to follow on from Luke, although it has been proposed that there may have been a predecessor to Luke in its present form, called "Proto-Luke" which would date Acts earlier. Some scholars date Acts very soon after Paul's detention in Rome (AD 60-62).[113]

This is significant dating. Since the Crucifixion happened around AD 30, the dates of the documents that describe the life of Jesus and the events immediately after his death were written well within the lifetime of those who observed the events, and of some of the Apostles. Think about events that happened 35 years ago—if you were to try to falsify the history many people would correct you.

Synoptic Gospels and Acts

The first three gospels: Matthew, Mark and Luke, contain a lot of common content, sometimes using identical words and passages. Because of this commonality they are called "Synoptic Gospels"; synoptic meaning "to take a common view."

The frequency of identical passages shows that the accounts were not written by three independent authors writing from scratch. Clearly some authors used the other's work for part of their documents. So, for instance, where there are identical passages in Mark and Matthew, either Mark wrote them first and Matthew copied the passage, or vice versa, or both of them copied the passage from a third source.

---

[113] *The New Testament Documents, Are they Reliable* by F.F. Bruce ISBN 978-1604598667

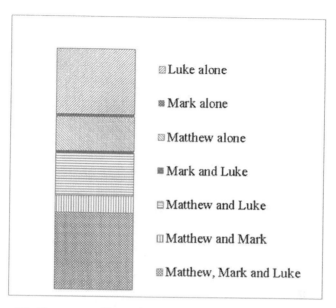

Luke alone

Mark alone

Matthew alone

Mark and Luke

Matthew and Luke

Matthew and Mark

Matthew, Mark and Luke

Figure 26. Commonality of passages in the Synoptic Gospels

The Gospel of Mark is traditionally thought to have documented the teaching of the apostle Peter, and so in the example above, the passages common to Mark and Matthew are believed to have been written by Mark, writing what he was told by Peter. Strong evidence for this comes from references made in other more recent documents. Eusebius of Caesarea (ca. AD 263–339) was a Roman historian. In his *Ecclesiastical History* he quotes from a five-volume treatise, *An Exposition of the Lord's Reports* by Papias, Bishop of Hierapolis in Phyrgia (ca. AD 60-130):

> *And the presbyter would say this: Mark, who had indeed been Peter's interpreter, accurately wrote as much as he remembered, yet not in order, about that which was either said or did by the Lord. For he neither heard the Lord nor followed him, but later, as I said, Peter, who would make the teachings anecdotally but not exactly an arrangement of the Lord's reports, so that Mark did not fail by writing certain things as he recalled. For he had one purpose, not to omit what he heard or falsify them.*

Mark is thought to be the John Mark referred to in the Book of Acts of the Apostles who accompanied Paul on some of his journeys.

This seems a quite reasonable explanation and description of Mark's Gospel; the capturing of eyewitness stories of many of the events of Jesus' life, not necessary in correct chronological order, but recorded as accurately as could be remembered. There is no inference that any of the accounts have been fabricated.

Given the source of Mark, we can conclude that both Matthew and Luke draw heavily on Mark. However, they also have new material. There is some material common to Matthew and Luke implying at least one other common source, and additional material in Matthew alone and material specific to Luke. There are many different theories about the sources for Matthew and Luke. Around 1900 a second major source for the gospels was proposed, called "Q", and this has subsequently been a foundation for biblical scholarship. "Q" was supposedly written in Greek. However, there is doubt about whether "Q" actually existed as a specific document (under another name of course) as no manuscript or fragment has been found that would match the content, and such a document has not been referred to in any of the old documents or church catalogues.

However, even if "Q" never existed as a circulated document there is evidence in the Greek of the "Q" material that it has been translated from Aramaic. Thus the real "Q" material may have been an Aramaic document or it may have come from an Aramaic oral tradition. The latter suggestion is supported by a further quotation from Papias, Bishop of Hierapolis where he states that:

> Matthew compiled the logia [sayings] in the Hebrew
> [Aramaic] language, and each one translated as best
> he could

The term logia refers to a compilation (or compilations) of the sayings of Jesus, which would have been in Aramaic (also referred to as Hebrew). Corroborating evidence for there being an Aramaic set of "sayings of Jesus" comes from fragments of parchment written in

Coptic (early Egyptian) and fragments written in Greek; the style and content in both Greek and Coptic implies both are translations from an Aramaic source.

This seems to imply that the extra material in Matthew may have been translated directly from the Aramaic, and that an intermediate document "Q" is not necessary. We can infer a well-established Aramaic oral tradition of sayings, and it is reasonable to suppose that these sayings passed the accuracy test; eyewitnesses would have been around to challenge any mistakes. Would the sayings have been word for word what Jesus said, or would they be paraphrasing? It probably doesn't matter. It is likely that Jesus taught the same message many times and perhaps with slightly different words, and so the sayings would be an accurate representation of what he taught even if not an absolutely identical set of words.

However, the Scandinavian Scholar, Birger Gerhardsson relates how rabbis in the second century AD taught their disciples memory techniques that allowed them to remember teaching that they had heard word for word[114]. These techniques may well have been around in the first century too, and so it is possible that the *"logia,"* the sayings of Jesus in Matthew and Luke, may be word for word what Jesus said.

There are many long speeches in the documents that Luke wrote, particularly in Acts, and he may have followed the approach of the Greek historian Thucydides:

> *"As to the speeches that were made by different men, either when they were about to begin the war or when they were already engaged therein, it has been difficult to recall with strict accuracy the words actually spoken, both for me as regards that which I myself heard, and for those who from various other sources have brought me reports. Therefore the*

---

[114] *Memory and Manuscript: Oral Tradition and written Transmission in Rabbinic Judaism and Early Christianity* Birger Gerhardsson ISBN 978-0802843661

speeches are given in the language in which, as it seemed to me, the several speakers would express, on the subjects under consideration, the sentiments most befitting the occasion, though at the same time 1 have adhered as closely as possible to the general sense of what was actually said." (Hist. 1.22.1)[115]

In the Book of Acts, there are many references to "we" in the text which indicate that the author was himself an eyewitness to the events. This is further supported by "we" not being used everywhere; the author clearly conveys that there were some events that he witnessed and others that he didn't.

In summary, there is a very good evidence to suggest that the accounts in Matthew, Mark and Luke accurately record what people of the day saw and heard Jesus saying and doing, even if some of the dialogue may not be word for word, and that the Book of Acts also accurately records events immediately after Jesus' death and resurrection.

The Gospel of John

Scholars agree that the Gospel of John was written later than the other gospels. It describes itself as an eyewitness account of the events of the life of Jesus. It is generally agreed that this Gospel was written by the apostle John. However, there is suggestion that the version we have today was not the first edition. The very oldest fragment of a New Testament document—the Rylands Library Papyrus P52, comes from the Gospel of John—is shown below:

---

[115]http://archive.org/stream/thucydideswithen01thucuoft/thucydid eswithen01thucuoft_djvu.txt accessed 23/6/13

Figure 27. Rylands fragment P52

Clearly the fragment is written on both sides, and from the style of writing it is dated at around AD 125, perhaps 30 years after the first edition was written.[116]

As an example of how one might examine an ancient text, researcher Ronald Price notes that

> 'The apparent inconsistencies in order in the text have led a variety of scholars to propose that a few passages have been displaced from their original positions. Many have commented on the fact that the supposedly displaced passages are mostly (if not all) close to multiples of 800 Greek letters in length.'

He then develops an approach to analysing the document based on that assumption:

> This investigation was based on the hypothesis that the apparent units of whole multiples of approximately 800 letters in many Gospel episodes

---

[116]http://www.library.manchester.ac.uk/searchresources/guidetosp ecialcollections/stjohnfragment/ accessed 26/3/13

are significant and can be explained as resulting from the particular way in which the author(s) used their papyrus sheets.

An initial assessment shows that whilst many of the sections we have today would fit that page size, there are some which don't. Some sections appear to be the wrong length; they don't fit the page pattern. Price suggests that the sections that don't fit may be later additions. From the sequence of the narrative he speculates that some sections may have got out of order.

Price proposes the hypothesis that a "First Edition" was originally written in three "acts" and allocates sections to each act.

Act 1: chs. 1-4 , 6 The messengers of God come down from Heaven

Act 2 chs. 7-12   The light of the world

Act 3 chs. 13-14 , 17-20   Jesus prepares to return to the Father in Heaven.[117]

From a mix of considering such simple things as numbers of characters on a page, it is possible to identify potential changes made to an original document. The style of writing in a given document may also hint at later additions. In addition to relatively robust analytical approaches, researchers appear to apply more speculative statements in their assessment of the documents. There is much less precision and agreement than one would find with a physics experiment for example. Nevertheless, this type of work demonstrates that the historical accuracy of the New Testament is remarkably traceable for such old documents.

---

[117] http://homepage.virgin.net/ron.price/john_home.html and other linked pages, accessed 9/6/13

Apocryphal Gospels

Matthew, Mark, Luke and John are called "canonical" gospels. We sometimes hear of other documents, "lost gospels" that are omitted from the Bible.

Dan Brown's book *The Da Vinci Code* claims that the Gospel of Philip describes a sexual relationship between Jesus and Mary Magdalene.[118] Why isn't that in the Bible? And aren't there other gospels that are omitted? Here again, we can benefit from the work of biblical scholars who know of all the available manuscripts, and who study the detailed construction of the documents.

The four gospels in the Bible are supported by a wealth of manuscripts, including translations into many languages. This is not the case with the "non-canonical" gospels. The Gospel of Philip is supported by very little manuscript evidence, and appears to have been written 100-200 years after the canonical gospels. The manuscript is incomplete, and the sexual innuendo in the Gospel of Philip is arrived at by filling in the spaces between the words "and __ companion of the __ Mary Magdalene __ used to __ more than the disciples __ greet her __ times the rest __." [119]

There are intriguingly simple approaches to analysing whether the gospels were really eyewitness accounts. Imagine that I, living in England decide to write a "history" of Nelson Mandela's life, and that it would be impractical for me to travel to South Africa to research the topic. I might gather some of the stories of what he did, perhaps from those who've been there, or from books that others had written on the topic. However, if I wanted to add some extra content then I would be at a distinct disadvantage because of my lack of detailed geographic knowledge. I might be able to refer to places like Johannesburg and Soweto that I'd heard of, but I wouldn't be

---

[118] Dan Brown: *The Da Vinci Code* – ISBN 978-0752100401

[119] "Evidence of History" Dr. Simon J. Gathercole. *The Authentic Gospels: New Evidence*, St Helen's Bishopsgate, London, June 2010

able to include any of the little villages or even describe particular houses or geographic features.

Scholars find that the "non-canonical" Gospel accounts that date from the first or second century are very short on geographical detail. In the four gospels there are twenty-two place names mentioned, but the non-canonical gospels only mention Jerusalem. The level of detail in the canonical gospels is consistent with eyewitness accounts, and the lack of local geographical detail in the non-canonical gospels suggests that they were later biographies and lacking eyewitness validity.[120]

We also learn that the way that people referred to Jesus changed over time. Later references speak more of his title than his name. An eyewitness, or a personal friend who had spent a lot of time with Jesus would more naturally have used his name "Jesus" when talking about him. In the canonical gospels we find phrases like *"Indignant because Jesus had healed on the Sabbath, the synagogue ruler said . . . ,"* and *"whilst Jesus was teaching in the temple."* Further, since Jesus was a common name, when addressing Jesus in a speech or similar it would be normal to put some further clarification as to which Jesus was being spoken to or about. Today we would use the full name Jesus Christ, but in the four canonical gospels we find that the clarification of the name might be Jesus of Nazareth, Jesus Son of David, and the demon possessed man shouts *"Jesus, Son of the Most High God."* Yet in the non-canonical gospels there is rare use of Jesus' name, he is referred to as Christ, Lord and even Saviour.

It has been claimed (in *The Da Vinci Code*, for example) that the selection of the four gospels was only made at the First Council of Nicaea (AD 325) but detailed examination shows that this is not true[121]. Iranaeus in the second century referred to the gospels Matthew, Mark, Luke and John in his writings; it seems that they were well established as the authoritative sources at that time.

---

[120] "Evidence of Eyewitnesses" Dr Peter J Williams *The Authentic Gospels: New Evidence*, St Helen's Bishopsgate, London, June 2010

[121] http://www.tertullian.org/rpearse/nicaea.html, accessed 9/6/13

The Letters

There are twenty-one letters in the New Testament. Many are identified as having been written by the apostles Paul, Peter, and John. One is from James and one from Jude, both brothers of Jesus. As one might expect, the letters contain greetings, general and specific teaching, and correction of misunderstanding.

There are conflicting views on their authorship and date; for example the following table indicates the spread of opinion about the letters of Paul:

Epistle	Conservative Christian Beliefs		Liberal Christian Beliefs	
	Date Written	Author	Date Written	Author
Romans	AD 55-56	Paul	AD 55-59 (Ch.1-15)	Paul
1 Corinthians	AD 54-55	Paul	>AD 55	Paul
2 Corinthians	AD 55-56	Paul	>AD 55	Paul
Galatians	AD 48	Paul	AD 48-62	Paul
Ephesians	AD 61	Paul	<AD 95	Unknown
Philippians	AD 62	Paul	AD 54-62	Paul
Colossians	AD 61	Paul	AD 54-90	Probably Paul
1 Thessalonians	AD 51	Paul	AD 50-51	Paul
2 Thessalonians	AD 51	Paul	AD 75-90	Unknown
1 Timothy	AD 62	Paul	AD 100-150	Unknown
2 Timothy	AD 64	Paul	AD 100-150	Unknown
Titus	AD 63	Paul	AD 100-150	Unknown
Philemon	AD 61	Paul	59-62	Paul

There is general agreement that some, if not all, date from within 30 years of the crucifixion, and so it is safe to conclude that they give a good and accurate understanding of the earliest Christian life and beliefs.

The Book of Revelation

There is a peculiar book at the end of the New Testament that includes various prophecies and strange imagery, and describes an apocalyptic end to the world and its replacement by a "New Jerusalem." It claims to be a record of a prophetic vision given to the author. It is thought to have been written between AD 70 and 95.[122]

Evidence of Other Contemporary Writers

Around the time of Christ and before Jerusalem fell to the Romans in AD 70, most of the Jewish law was passed on in the verbal tradition. However, after the fall of Jerusalem various rabbis started to write down the case law, compiling the Mishnah. This then became the subject of study and a commentary was compiled called the Gemara. The Mishnah and Gemara combined are the Talmud. The Jewish Talmud was completed around AD 300. It contains reference to Jesus. FF Bruce describes that:

> *According to the earlier rabbis whose opinions are recorded in these writings, Jesus of Nazareth was a transgressor in Israel, who practices magic, scorned the words of the wise, led the people astray, and said he had not come to destroy the law but to add to it. He was hanged on Passover Eve for heresy and misleading the people. His disciples, of whom five are named, healed the sick in his name.*[123]

An earlier independent record comes from the Jewish historian Josephus. After a somewhat colourful life he befriended the Romans, taking the family name Flavius and becoming known as Flavius Josephus. He wrote several books, and many of his narratives reflect closely the descriptions of events found in the gospels, for example the death of Herod Agrippa.

---

[122] http://www.ecclesia.org/truth/revelation.html accessed 23/6/13
[123] *The New Testament Documents, Are they Reliable* by F.F. Bruce
ISBN 978-1604598667

About Jesus, he writes:

> *And there arose about this time Jesus, a wise man,* ***if***
> ***indeed we should call him a man,*** *for he was a*
> *doer of marvellous deeds, a teacher of men who*
> *receive the truth with pleasure. He led away many*
> *Jews, and also many of the Greeks.* ***This man was***
> ***the Christ.*** *And when Pilate had condemned him to*
> *the cross on his impeachment by the chief men among*
> *us, those who had loved him at first did not cease;* ***for***
> ***he appeared to them on the third day alive***
> ***again, the divine prophets having spoken these***
> ***and thousands of other wonderful things about***
> ***him:*** *and even now the tribe of Christians, so named*
> *after him, has not yet died out.'*

There is some controversy about the bold phrases; are they
original or were they added to the text in later copying? The passage
is referenced in Origen (185-254 AD) an early Christian writer, who
tells us that Josephus did not believe Jesus to be the Messiah or call
him such. This would seem to conflict with the bold phrases.
However, even if one treats the bold phrases with caution, the
evidence is corroboration of the related parts of the Gospel
narratives.

There are also references in non-Jewish writings to Christ and
his followers.

A Syrian named Mara Bar-Serapion writing from prison to his
son Serapion included the following passage:

> *What advantage did the Athenians gain from putting*
> *Socrates to death? Famine and plague came upon*
> *them as a judgement for their crime. What advantage*
> *did the men of Samos gain from burning Pythagoras?*
> *In a moment their land was covered with sand. What*
> *advantage did the Jews gain from executing their*
> *wise King? It was just after that their Kingdom was*
> *abolished. God justly avenged these three wise men:*

the Athenians died of hunger; the Samians were overwhelmed by the sea; the Jews, ruined and driven from their land, live in complete dispersion. But Socrates did not die for good; he lived on in the teaching of Plato. Pythagoras did not die for good; he lived on in the statue of Hera. Nor did the wise King die for good; He lived on in the teaching which He had given.[124]

Some question when this was written (between AD 73 and AD 200 probably) and also the accuracy as there is doubt as to whether Pythagoras was burnt, or what the statue of Hera refers to.

The Roman historian Cornelius Tacitus, writing probably around AD 110 about the fire in Rome in AD 64 tells that:

But not all the relief that could come from man, not all the bounties that the prince could bestow, nor all the atonements which could be presented to the gods, availed to relieve Nero from the infamy of being believed to have ordered the conflagration, the fire of Rome. Hence to suppress the rumour, he falsely charged with the guilt, and punished Christians, who were hated for their enormities. Christus, the founder of the name, was put to death by Pontius Pilate, procurator of Judea in the reign of Tiberius: but the pernicious superstition, repressed for a time broke out again, not only through Judea, where the mischief originated, but through the city of Rome also. Annals XV,44[125]

---

[124] http://www.earlychristianwritings.com/mara.html accessed 23/6/13

[125] http://www.agapebiblestudy.com/documents/Historical%20evidence%20on%20the%20exhistance%20of%20Jesus.htm accessed 23/6/13

In AD 112 Plinius Secundus (Pliny the Younger), governor of Pontus and Bithynia from 111-113 wrote the following letter to the Emperor Trajan of Rome:

It is a rule, Sir, which I inviolably observe, to refer myself to you in all my doubts; for who is more capable of guiding my uncertainty or informing my ignorance? Having never been present at any trials of the Christians, I am unacquainted with the method and limits to be observed either in examining or punishing them. Whether any difference is to be allowed between the youngest and the adult; whether repentance admits to a pardon, or if a man has been once a Christian it avails him nothing to recant; whether the mere profession of Christianity, albeit without crimes, or only the crimes associated therewith are punishable -- in all these points I am greatly doubtful.

In the meanwhile, the method I have observed towards those who have denounced to me as Christians is this: I interrogated them whether they were Christians; if they confessed it I repeated the question twice again, adding the threat of capital punishment; if they still persevered, I ordered them to be executed. For whatever the nature of their creed might be, I could at least feel no doubt that contumacy and inflexible obstinacy deserved chastisement. There were others also possessed with the same infatuation, but being citizens of Rome, I directed them to be carried thither.

These accusations spread (as is usually the case) from the mere fact of the matter being investigated and several forms of the mischief came to light. A placard was put up, without any signature, accusing a large number of persons by name. Those who denied they were, or had ever been, Christians, who repeated after me an invocation to the gods, and offered adoration, with wine and frankincense, to your image, which I had ordered to be brought for that purpose, together with those of the gods, and who finally cursed Christ -- none of which acts, it is into performing -- these I thought it proper to discharge. Others who were named by that informer at first confessed themselves Christians, and then denied it; true, they had been of that persuasion but they had quitted it, some three years, others many years, and a few as much as twenty-five years ago. They all worshipped your statue and the images of the gods, and cursed Christ.

They affirmed, however, the whole of their guilt, or their error, was, that they were in the habit of meeting on a certain fixed day before it was light, when they sang in alternate verses a hymn to Christ, as to a god, and bound themselves by a solemn oath, not to any wicked deeds, but never to commit any fraud, theft, or adultery, never to falsify their word, nor deny a trust when they should be called upon to deliver it up; after which it was their custom to separate, and then reassemble to partake of food -- but food of an ordinary and innocent kind. Even this practice, however, they had abandoned after the publication of my edict, by which, according to your orders, I had forbidden political associations. I judged it so much the more necessary to extract the real truth, with the assistance of torture, from two female slaves, who were styled deaconesses: but I could discover nothing more than depraved and excessive superstition.

I therefore adjourned the proceedings, and betook myself at once to your counsel. For the matter seemed to me well worth referring to you, especially *considering the numbers endangered. Persons of all ranks and ages, and of both sexes are, and will be, involved in the prosecution. For this contagious superstition is not confined to the cities only, but has spread through the villages and rural districts; it seems possible, however, to check and cure it.*[126]

I find the description of their crime intriguing (as I have highlighted in bold above).

Further Evidence

According to Luke when Jesus was praying in the Garden of Gethsemane before his arrest, trial and crucifixion he was extremely anxious and was sweating blood.

> *He prayed more fervently, and he was in such agony of spirit that his sweat fell to the ground like great drops of blood. Luke 22:44*

This is now known to be a clinical condition called hematidrosis, associated with extreme stress. The following abstract is taken from a study reported in 1996 in the Journal of Medicine:

> *In order to verify the accuracy of the commonly used statement, "I sweat blood," a survey of the literature in the subject of hematidrosis was made. Seventy-six cases were studied and classified into categories according to the causative factor. These were: component of systemic disease, vicarious menstruation, excessive exertion, psychogenic, and unknown. The psychogenic were further subdivided into those that occurred only one time, those that recurred and the stigmatics. Acute fear and intense mental contemplation were found to be the most frequent inciting causes. Hematidrosis is an extremely rare clinical phenomenon with only few*

---

[126] <u>Pagan Rome and the Early Christians</u> Stephen Benko ISBN 978-0713448009

instances reported to have occurred within the twentieth century.[127]

It seems reasonable to suppose that Jesus did indeed sweat blood, and that Luke accurately recorded something that was unusual and inexplicable at the time.

The gospels also record that:

> *One of the soldiers, however, pierced his side with a spear, and immediately blood and water flowed out. (This report is from an eyewitness giving an accurate account. He speaks the truth so that you also can believe.) These things happened in fulfilment of the Scriptures that say, "Not one of his bones will be broken," and "They will look on the one they pierced." John 19:34-37*

The following describes what might have happened.

> *The Roman flogging or scourging that Jesus endured prior to being crucified normally consisted of 39 lashes, but could have been more (Mark 15:15; John 19:1). The whip that was used, called a flagrum, consisted of braided leather thongs with metal balls and pieces of sharp bone woven into or intertwined with the braids. The balls added weight to the whip, causing deep bruising and contusions as the victim was struck. The pieces of bone served to cut into the flesh. As the beating continued, the resulting cuts were so severe that the skeletal muscles, underlying veins, sinews, and bowels of victims were exposed. This beating was so severe that at times victims would not survive it in order to go on to be crucified.*
>
> *Those who were flogged would often go into hypovolemic shock, a term that refers to low blood*

[127] "Blood, Sweat, and Fear. A Classification of Hematidrosis" Holoubek, J.E. and A.B. Holoubek *Journal of Medicine*(1996), 27[3-4]:115-33.

volume. In other words, the person would have lost so much blood he would go into shock. The results of this would be

1) The heart would race to pump blood that was not there.

2) The victim would collapse or faint due to low blood pressure.

3) The kidneys would shut down to preserve body fluids.

4) The person would experience extreme thirst as the body desired to replenish lost fluids.

There is evidence from scripture that Jesus experienced hypovolemic shock as a result of being flogged. As Jesus carried His own cross to Golgotha (John 19:17), He collapsed, and a man named Simon was forced to either carry the cross or help Jesus carry the cross the rest of way to the hill (Matthew 27:32–33; Mark 15:21–22; Luke 23:26). This collapse indicates Jesus had low blood pressure. Another indicator that Jesus suffered from hypovolemic shock was that He declared He was thirsty as He hung on the cross (John 19:28), indicating His body's desire to replenish fluids.

Prior to death, the sustained rapid heartbeat caused by hypovolemic shock also causes fluid to gather in the sack around the heart and around the lungs. This gathering of fluid in the membrane around the heart is called pericardial effusion, and the fluid gathering around the lungs is called pleural effusion. This explains why, after Jesus died and a Roman soldier thrust a spear through Jesus' side (probably His right side, piercing both the lungs and the heart), blood and water came from His side just as John recorded in his Gospel (John 19:34).[128]

Of course, this medical knowledge would not have been available at the time, but John is at pains to convince the reader that this really happened, implying that it was surprising and unusual. We are left in no doubt that Jesus suffered great distress and died on the cross.

In Conclusion

We cannot doubt that Jesus Christ existed. The gospels are a reliable historical source that can be traced back to specific eyewitnesses to the events. Through the written Greek and Coptic we can see that passages record the spoken Aramaic tradition. Whilst the speeches may not be recorded word for word, we can confidently take them as conveying what was communicated, and take the events described as accurate descriptions of what eyewitnesses saw happening.

We can infer a lot from the behaviour of the participants. There was dramatic change in the behaviour of the disciples following Jesus' death and reported resurrection. Clearly something profound happened to change their courage and character.

After Jesus' crucifixion, his followers were convinced that he had been raised from the dead. The disciples became the leaders of a new movement that has grown into the Christian religion that thrives today.

Initially, the disciples would have been able to teach in person what they had seen, and what Jesus had taught. The followers were geographically closely located and there would have been no need for books and documents. However, as time passed and the

---

[128] http://www.gotquestions.org/blood-water-Jesus.html accessed 9/6/13

movement grew, it would be necessary to preserve and communicate the message to many more people, in many places.

In the early stages this could be done by personal visits, by spending time with each community. Paul completed three missionary journeys, visiting many cities and teaching the people in person. The letters of the New Testament were written to reinforce the verbal messages that Paul had given to new believers, and these letters are amongst the earliest documents. Following his visits, letters would be the only means available to Paul to communicate directly over a large distance.

The central message needed to be communicated consistently, and so a set of "sayings" was developed. These sayings, the Loggia, initially followed the oral tradition. The description of what Jesus did was written down due the danger of the events passing from living memory as the eyewitnesses reached old age. Of the Gospel accounts, the earliest, Mark focuses more on what Jesus did, whereas Matthew and Luke contain more of what he said, incorporating the Loggia.

The New Testament contains a high quality set of historical documents that describe the actions and message that Jesus of Nazareth brought to the world. In view of the good provenance of the documents, it is reasonable to conclude that the contents are reliable.

The most rational conclusion of who Jesus was and what he did is that which is recorded in the gospels. Jesus was crucified and died, and by the next but one day his tomb was empty. We can conclude that his body was neither taken by his disciples, nor by his opponents—both would have behaved differently and produced Jesus' body if they had taken it. The rational explanation is that he was no longer there, and that he had not been removed by human hand.

It is recorded that after the crucifixion Jesus appeared in physical form to many of his followers at different times and places. His followers were dramatically changed and spiritually empowered, and were no longer a frightened group that had just witnessed the crucifixion of their leader.

If we are not prepared to accept the possibility that God exists then we need to find alternative explanations for all of these historical facts.

I conclude that Jesus lived, performed miracles, taught great wisdom, was crucified, came back to life two days later and met with his followers. On the basis of the evidence of his miraculous deeds, I conclude that Jesus spoke for God.

What Has Changed Since Jesus Time?

Over the years religion has been used to reinforce many a leader's position of power, enabling him to control people. This has happened at times within the Christian religion too.

Initially Christianity was an underground movement. We read earlier about followers of Christ that:

> the whole of their guilt, or their error, was, that they were in the habit of meeting on a certain fixed day before it was light, when they sang in alternate verses a hymn to Christ, as to a god, and bound themselves by a solemn oath, not to any wicked deeds, but never to commit any fraud, theft, or adultery, never to falsify their word, nor deny a trust when they should be called upon to deliver it up

The first 300 years saw Christians active in spreading the message, flavoured with martyrdom. Local religious and political leaders didn't like this new faith in a God of grace and forgiveness undermining their control of the people, and hence Christians lived in danger of death. This was particularly so in the Roman Empire; Nero was very adept at "punishment" of the early Christians with extreme cruelty.[129] Yet there are many genuine records that show that these Christians were happy to go to their deaths, certain that the temporary suffering was as nothing compared to the promised eternal life with Christ.[130]

There were factions who interpreted the gospels in accordance with their differing worldviews; for instance some claimed that continuing to live immoral lives before asking for forgiveness made God's grace even more magnificent.[131] Many of the conclusions came to be adopted into the doctrines of mainline Christianity, including such issues as the Trinity: God as Father, Son and Holy Spirit.

Circa AD 310 the emperor Constantine adopted Christianity as the state religion of the Roman Empire. He did not want a disorderly religion, and convened the Council of Nicaea in AD 325 to force the Christian leaders of the day to reach a conclusion on many contentious issues. He wanted a clear definition of what Christianity was, and what a follower should believe. The "brand" was established, and was very effectively distributed around the empire in the centuries to come.

Unfortunately religion was now closely linked with the state and so religious leaders and state leaders vied for power. The power

---

[129] http://www.eyewitnesstohistory.com/christians.htm accessed 10/6/13

[130] "Letter from the colony of God's church at SMYRNA to the colony of God's church at PHILOMELIUM." In *Early Christian Writings* translated by Maxwell Staniforth. ISBN 0-14-044475

[131] Romans 6

of the Pope was enormous, but the quality of person did not always match the requirements of the position. In the 15th century Girolamo Savonaola commented that "The temporal power of the Pope is at the bottom of all the evils and abuses which have slipped in to the church."[132]

The Bible itself was a rare commodity, each copy having been painstakingly copied by hand. It was not in the native language of most people; a priest was necessary to interpret it. Again, the scope for manipulation (whether intentional or not) and judgement of others was enormous. Heretics would be driven out and burned. Fear and superstition led to atrocities and victimisation of the "strange." Individuals were accused of being witches and bizarre tests invented to prove if they were.[133] Christian principles were sacrificed to political requirement. Good and evil battled within the corridors of power and within the church.[134]

But in the midst of all the politicking and blundering there remained a central core of desire to do what was right, and to follow the message of Jesus.

With the translation of the Bible into native languages (in the 14th century in England), the people could begin to learn directly what it meant to follow Jesus. They could begin to read and interpret the gospels for themselves, and leaders could no longer manipulate them in the name of God. Theological rebellions such as that of the Puritan movement removed many of the excesses introduced by opulent church leaders, and the infallibility of the Pope was challenged. Preachers such as Wesley travelled thousands of miles to preach Christ's message of forgiveness and love to the people.

---

[132] *AD 2000 years of Christianity* edited by Christopher Howse ISBN 0-281-05287-5

[133] http://salem.lib.virginia.edu/home.html accessed 10/6/13

[134] *Black Robes in Paraguay: The Success of the Guarani Missions Hastened the Abolition of the Jesuits* William F. Jaenike ISBN 978-1933794044, (and the movie "The Mission")

In Georgian and through to Victorian times churchgoing was the cultural rock on which society functioned. Hard work, going to church and patriotism were the values of the day. Yet the Sunday churchgoer still drove his workforce to more profits during the week, or manned the slave ships that took the workforce to the plantations. Such "Cultural Christianity" was challenged by the likes of William Wilberforce, whose book *Real Christianity* pointed out the hypocrisy of many of those churchgoers.[135] Contrast with today, when churchgoing is "un-cool" and anti-cultural. Fewer people go to church, often only for weddings and funerals, yet I wonder if the number of "true" Christians has varied much over the years.

I sometimes wonder what Jesus thinks of the state of the world today. Yet he didn't concern himself with the world but with people's hearts, and with their relationship with God and with each other. What is clear is that the battle between good and evil continues, although weapons may have changed. Comfort and boredom have deadened recent generations and led us into passivity, allowing evil to thrive. Extreme poverty, corruption, injustice, slavery and other ills continue to flourish whilst good men and women sit in front of the TV and "tut-tut" about the state of things. It is time to remember the words of Martin Luther King:

> "The greatest sins of our time are committed not by
> the few who have destroyed, but by the vast majority
> who sat idly by."

---

[135] *Real Christianity* William Wilberforce ISBN 978-0830743117

Isn't that a message that Jesus proclaimed and endorsed through his life and death? Doesn't the world still need that underground movement of followers of Jesus today; a movement of "true" Christians? I think it does.

Logical Fallacy: "No True Scotsman"

The term was coined by Antony Flew, who gave an example of a Scotsman who sees a newspaper article about a series of sex crimes taking place in Brighton, and responds that "no Scotsman would do such a thing." When later confronted with evidence of another Scotsman doing even worse acts, his response is that "no true Scotsman would do such a thing," thus disavowing membership in the group "Scotsman" to the criminal on the basis that the commission of the crime is evidence for not being a Scotsman. However, this is a fallacy as there is nothing in the definition of "Scotsman" which makes such acts impossible. The term "No True Scotsman" has since expanded to refer to anyone who attempts to disown or distance themselves from wayward members of a group by excluding them from it.

Broadly speaking, the fallacy does not apply if there is a clear and well-understood definition of what membership in a group requires and it is that definition which is broken (e.g., "no honest man would lie like that!," "no Christian would worship

Chapter 7: God Has a Purpose for Each of Us

On Purpose

We are taught that we need to set personal goals, that we have to meet business targets, and that we need to save in order to achieve a comfortable retirement. We learn to think ahead, to plan, to "be prepared." Management gurus tell us to remember the five P's; Perfect Planning Prevents Poor Performance. We need all this planning, preparing and envisioning in order for our intelligent actions to achieve results, and yet some claim that the immensely complex and wonderful universe, that life, and that we are simply the result of a purposeless accident.

I would contend that everything we do is guided by purpose. I used to play cricket at a good standard; I reached the heights of playing three first class matches. When batting, I would be aware of the situation of the match; did I need to score runs quickly or did I need to simply protect my wicket? When the bowler bowled, my purpose guided the sort of shot that I would play. I would have no time to consciously think "I will play an off drive," or "I will play a forward defensive." I would have no chance to even consider which muscles to move in order to play the required stroke. Indeed, if the research is right that suggests that consciousness only begins half a second after the event it would be impossible for me to consciously choose what shot to play[136]. All that I could do would be to instil a purpose on the automatic behaviour of my body. Sometimes it would work, and I would play the sort of shot that I wanted, but all too often my "natural game" would take over and I'd attempt to hit the ball for four and get out in the process.

We see the same purposefulness in animals. Release a homing pigeon and it will, as the name suggests, fly home. If it gets blown off course, it will correct its direction. It knows its goal, its purpose and

---

[136] *Libet's Temporal Anomalies: A Reassessment of the Data* by Stanley A. Klein

it will alter its behaviour and actions to reach that goal. It doesn't have time to get out maps, take bearings, and consciously decide the best route, it may not even be capable of conscious thought. It just knows its goal and flies there by instinct.

The solitary wasp, Paralastor B, builds a nest in the ground with a trumpet-like entrance. The entrance is always a similar length and shape and the wasp works purposely to build the entrance. Whilst the wasp is away, if earth is placed around the straight part of the un-finished trumpet then the wasp will continue building the straight part until it reaches the usual length above ground, and then proceeds to build the trumpet shape. If part of the trumpet is broken the wasp will repair it. If a hole is made in part of the trumpet that cannot be repaired from inside, the wasp repairs it from the outside. But since the hole looks like the entrance in the earth to the nest, the wasp repairs it by building another trumpet on top. The wasp has a goal, a purpose, and it will unconsciously but intelligently carry out whatever actions are needed to fulfil that purpose.[137]

I discussed how a cell behaves with intelligence. The cell needs to know its purpose; "become a skin cell," or "become a nerve cell" for instance. The cell then carries out the necessary actions to fulfil that purpose.

The evolutionary process itself appears to follow a purpose. Remember convergent evolution; the camera eye that has evolved on many occasions[138]. There are many examples of such convergence on a common solution via different routes, consistent with a purpose-oriented process.

As an engineer I can understand that there are "perfect" designs that the natural selection process will seek out. In engineering there is, for instance, a perfect distribution of material in a turbine blade in order to achieve an optimum stress distribution.

---

[137] Rupert Sheldrake: *The Science Delusion* ISBN 978-1444727944 p136

[138] http://www.mapoflife.org/about/convergent_evolution/?section=0 accessed 3/3/13

Blades with the perfect distribution can withstand higher speeds than those which are not perfect. There is an inherent perfection in the nature of matter, and the evolutionary process seems perfectly designed to reach that perfection. Anything less than perfect is gradually eliminated.

Returning to the physical sciences, we can do our two slit experiment and we see that millions of photons shot at two slits form an interference pattern. Each photon produces one pinpoint on the screen, yet as a whole they produce a predictable pattern. We cannot predict where an individual photon will go, yet the photons purposefully work together to create the interference pattern.

In the above examples, there is only one case where we are aware that there is a conscious choice about the purpose or goal; in the cricket match when I would choose what sort of shot I want to play. It seems that humans are given the opportunity to choose our purpose. And in the same way that our conscious mind can give purpose to our complex body, we can appreciate that a greater conscious mind can give purpose to the rest of the universe.

Whilst much of the working of the universe and the appreciation of the non-material can be deduced by thought and experiment, this can never be sufficient to fully understand the character of God. There are some things that we can't work out and that God has had to reveal himself. That is the role of the Bible.

The Bible—a Source of Purpose

During my investigations for this book, examining the provenance of the biblical documents, looking at the discoveries of science, I have leaned towards a critical and analytical approach. I began to view the Bible in a similar way. I have seen preachers teaching one thing but doing another and I am embarrassed by invalid uses of the Bible, such as the Westborough Baptists. The Bible can be used for harm rather than for good, and as a weapon to attack those we find disagreeable. And I have a concern that some Christians seem to worship the Bible rather than God.

But then I realised with humility how important and valuable it is, particularly to those whose lives are so much harder than my own. In the novel *Uncle Tom's Cabin* an old slave, Tom, has been sold off to pay his owner's debts. We find him an old man, parted from his wife and children and the home where he's lived for decades, expecting to die under a harsh owner "down South," unable to communicate with his wife and children, never expecting to see them again. He is sitting on a bale of cotton, reading his Bible:

> *Is it strange, then, that some tears fall on the pages of his Bible, as he lays it on the cotton-bale, and, with patient finger, threading his slow way from word to word, traces out its promises? Having learned late in life, Tom was but a slow reader, and passed on laboriously from verse to verse. Fortunate for him was it that the book he was intent on was one which slow reading cannot injure, -- nay, one whose words, like ingots of gold, seem often to need to be weighed separately, that the mind may take in their priceless value. Let us follow him a moment, as, pointing to each word, and pronouncing each half aloud, he reads,*
>
> *"Let -- not -- your -- heart -- be -- troubled. In -- my -- Father's -- house -- are -- many -- mansions. I -- go-to -- prepare -- a -- place -- for -- you."*
>
> *Cicero, when he buried his darling and only daughter, had a heart as full of honest grief as poor Tom's, -- perhaps no fuller, for both were only men;- but Cicero could pause over no such sublime words of hope, and look to no such future reunion; and if he had seen them, ten to one he would not have believed, -- he must fill his head first with a thousand questions of authenticity of manuscript, and correctness of translation. But, to poor Tom, there it lay, just what he needed, so evidently true and divine that the possibility of a question never entered his simple*

head. It must be true; for, if not true, how could he live?[139]

The Bible is a wonderful book that has sustained those who are suffering, given hope to the hopeless and peace to the troubled. It has guided men and women through great acts of love and sacrifice. It is a book of very special importance.

What Does the New Testament Tell Us?

If we reflect on the enormous impact that Jesus has had on the world then we will realise that there was something special about him. It's worth finding out what he said and did. The best sources are the Gospel documents in the Bible, but I will summarise here.

Jesus didn't start to make his impact until he was around thirty years old. Things began when a man called John was baptising people. When Jesus was baptised John the Baptist declared that Jesus was the one sent by God. We read that

> *As he was praying, the heavens opened, and the Holy Spirit, in bodily form, descended on him like a dove. And a voice from Heaven said, "You are my dearly loved Son, and you bring me great joy." Luke 4:22*

This was the critical moment for Jesus; his affirmation of who he was and his call to start his work. The Gospel of Luke tells us that Jesus began by declaring that an old prophecy by Isaiah was now fulfilled:

> *"The spirit of the LORD is upon me, for he has anointed me to bring good news to the poor. He has sent me to proclaim that captives will be released, that the blind will see, that the oppressed will be set free, and that the time of the LORD's favour has come" Luke 4: 18-19*

---

[139] *Uncle Tom's Cabin* by Harriet Beecher Stowe. Published in 1852

In modern language that might be considered as his "mission statement." When the people of one town where he was teaching wanted him to stay he declared:

> "I must preach the Good News of the Kingdom of God
> in other towns, too, because that is why I was sent."
> Luke 4: 43

"Good News?" Not the message of oppression or regulation which is what religion has become in the eyes of many. As Luke continues, we see different themes emerging:

- Jesus demonstrating his authority: who he was, who his father was, and why he came
- Healing the sick and freeing them from their demons
- Teaching and demonstrating what God thinks of religion. Breaking religious rules of the day, particularly when they prevented people from performing acts of kindness or kept them from getting closer to God
- Living and teaching the right attitude to all aspects of life
- Being clear about what he expected from his followers and leading by example
- Living and teaching the paramount importance of love, and showing how to love others
- Living and teaching the importance of forgiveness and of not judging others
- Living and teaching how to relate to God

All of these come under the overriding umbrella of his mission statement; they are all Good News, they are all about healing and freedom, they are all about receiving the blessing of God. The following sections look at these themes in more detail.

Jesus Demonstrated His Authority and Why He Came

The first example in Luke of Jesus declaring who he was came as a child. His parents had lost him at the Passover festival, but eventually found him in the temple where he was:

. . . sitting among the religious leaders, listening to them and asking questions. All who heard him were amazed at his understanding and his answers. . . . His mother said to him " . . . Your father and I have been frantic, searching for you everywhere." "But why did you need to search?" he asked. "Didn't you know that I must be in my Father's house?" Luke 2: 48-49

We quickly read an example of Jesus demonstrating his authority and spiritual power:

Once when he was in the synagogue, a man possessed by a demon — an evil spirit — began shouting at Jesus, "Go away! Why are you interfering with us, Jesus of Nazareth? Have you come to destroy us? I know who you are — the Holy One sent from God!" Jesus cut him short. "Be quiet! Come out of the man," he ordered. At that, the demon threw the man to the floor as the crowd watched; then it came out of him without hurting him further. Amazed, the people exclaimed, "What authority and power this man's words possess! Even evil spirits obey him, and they flee at this command!" Luke 4: 33-36

Jesus would often use miraculous healing to demonstrate his authority. The Oxford on-line dictionary defines authority as:

1. *the power or right to give orders , make decisions, and enforce obedience*

2. *a person or organisation having political or administrative power and control*

3. *the power to influence others , especially because of one's commanding manner or*

one's   recognised   knowledge   about
something[140]

Through different episodes Jesus showed all of these forms of authority. In particular he showed the religious leaders of the time that not only did he speak for God (as the prophets of earlier times had done) but that he had the authority of God. In one instance, a paralysed man had been brought to him wanting to be healed:

> Jesus said to the man, "Young man, your sins are forgiven." But the Pharisees and teachers of religious law said to themselves, "Who does he think he is? That's blasphemy! Only God can forgive sins!" Jesus knew what they were thinking so he asked them, "Why do you question this in your hearts? Is it easier to say 'Your sins are forgiven' or 'Stand up and walk'? So I will prove to you that the Son of Man has the authority on earth to forgive sins." Then Jesus turned to the paralysed man and said, "Stand up, pick up your mat, and go home!" And immediately, as everyone watched, the man jumped up, picked up his mat, and went home praising God. Luke 5: 20-25

It is events such as this that show the Jesus not only claimed but demonstrated that he had the authority of God. If the Pharisees were correct and that only God could forgive sins then this was saying that Jesus was God.

Jesus Healed the Sick and Freed Them from Their Demons

There were many people in Jesus time who were sick that he didn't heal, but he healed all those who asked. He was always compassionate, always ready to heal, but he didn't force healing on those who didn't want it. At times he encountered the ingratitude of those who were healed:

---

[140]http://oxforddictionaries.com/definition/english/authority?q=aut hority accessed 22/7/13

As he entered a village there, ten lepers stood at a distance, crying out, "Jesus, Master, have mercy on us!" He looked at them and said "Go show yourself to the priests." And as they went, they were cleansed of their leprosy. One of them, when he say that he was healed, came back to Jesus shouting, "Praise God!" He fell to the ground at Jesus feet, thanking him for what he had done. This man was a Samaritan. Jesus asked, "Didn't I heal ten men? Where are the other nine? Has no one returned to give glory to God except this foreigner?" Luke 17: 12-18

The recorded healings in Luke are:

- Demon-possessed man (Luke 4:33-35)
- Simon's mother-in-law, sick with high fever (Luke 4: 39)
- Sick villagers, all sorts of diseases and demon possessions (Luke 4: 40-41)
- Man with leprosy (Luke 5: 13)
- Paralysed man (Luke 5: 24)
- Man with deformed hand (Luke 6: 10)
- Many in the crowds (Luke 6: 19)
- Slave of a Roman officer (Luke 7: 9-10)
- Dead son of a widow brought back to life (Luke 7: 14-15)
- Another demon-possessed man (Luke 8: 27-33)
- Woman who had suffered from constant bleeding (Luke 8: 48)
- Dead daughter of Jairus brought back to life (Luke 8: 54-55)
- Those who were sick in the crowd (Luke 9: 11)
- Demon-possessed boy (Luke 9: 41-42)
- Woman who had been bent double for eighteen years (Luke 13: 8)
- Man whose arms and legs were swollen with dropsy (Luke 14 :4)
- Ten lepers (Luke 17: 12-18)
- Blind beggar (Luke 18: 42)
- The ear of a soldier come to arrest him, after it was slashed off (Luke 22: 51)

Jesus Taught and Demonstrated What God Thinks of Religion

In Jesus' time there was a very active and powerful priesthood led by the Pharisees. It was good business to be a priest; they held power over the people by telling them what God wanted them to do and how to behave. There was money to be made by judging what was acceptable as a sacrifice to God: it had to be one that you bought from the Pharisees and you had to pay in special temple money because ordinary money was unclean, and you had to change your ordinary money into temple money at the priest's money-change booth.

Jesus was extremely angry with the practice of selling "acceptable" sacrifices in the temple:

> *Then Jesus entered the Temple and began to drive out the people selling animals for sacrifices. He said to them, "The scriptures declare, 'My Temple will be a house of prayer,' but you have turned it into a den of thieves." Luke 19: 45-46*

There are many examples of Jesus breaking religious rules of the day when they kept people from acts of kindness or from getting closer to God. The Pharisees had a problem with Jesus:

> *The Pharisees and their teachers of religious law complained bitterly to Jesus' disciples. "Why do you eat and drink with such scum?" Jesus answered them "Healthy people don't need a doctor —sick people do. I have come to call not those who think they are righteous, but those who know they are sinners and need to repent." Luke 5: 30-32*

The Pharisees were very particular about not working on the Sabbath and had carefully defined rules of what constituted work. Jesus wanted to show them that there are things more important than strict observance of the law. He would often heal someone on the Sabbath, which angered the Pharisees, but he would use the event to try to teach them compassion and love:

206

One Sabbath day Jesus went to eat dinner in the
home of a leader of the Pharisees and the people were
watching him closely. There was a man there whose
arms and legs were swollen. Jesus asked the Pharisees
and experts in religious law, "Is it permitted in the
law to heal people on the Sabbath day, or not? " When
they refused to answer, Jesus touched the sick man
and healed him and sent him away. Then he turned
to them and said, "Which of you doesn't work on the
Sabbath? If your son or your cow falls into a pit,
don't you rush to get him out?" Again they could not
answer. Luke 14: 1-6

Another time the Pharisees complained that Jesus' disciples
were breaking off the heads of some corn and eating the grain:

Some Pharisees said, "Why are you breaking the law
by harvesting grain on the Sabbath?" Jesus replied,
"Haven't you read in the scriptures what David did
when he and his companions were hungry? He went
into the house of God and broke the law by eating the
sacred loaves of bread that only the priests can eat.
He also gave some to his companions." And Jesus
added, "The Son of Man is Lord, even over the
Sabbath." Luke 6: 2-5

Jesus used the term Son of Man in the passage above, and
elsewhere, to refer to himself. He was therefore claiming to be Lord.

Another recorded event was a big dinner at the home of one
of the Pharisees. Jesus was invited, but he went straight in to eat
instead of carrying out the ceremonial washing that the Pharisees
insisted on. Jesus commented that:

"You Pharisees are so careful to clean the outside of
the cup and the dish, but inside you are filthy—full
of greed and wickedness! . . . What sorrow awaits you
experts in religious law! For you crush people with

207

unbearable religious demands, and you never life a
finger to ease the burden" Luke 11: 39, 46

These are all examples of Jesus showing what was wrong with their religious practices, but he also spoke clearly about what was needed.

Jesus Lived and Taught the Right Attitude to All Aspects of Life

Jesus teaches a lot through parables, many of which are recorded in Luke, but also he teaches directly. He tells us to love our enemies and be good to those who hate us, to give to anyone who asks, to lend without expecting repayment. Why? Because if we do, we will keep bitterness from our heart.

He tells us not to worry about everyday life—whether we have enough food or clothes:

"Can all your worries add a single moment to your
life?" Luke 12: 25

He tells us to have honest humility. He describes a meal where the most important people take the top places at the table. He tells us not to go high up the table, because someone more important might come and we would be sent lower down and suffer disgrace. Far better to take a seat lower down and be called up higher. And he also advises us not to become too self-confident or arrogant in our dealings with God:

"Two men went to the temple to pray. One was a
Pharisee, and the other was a despised tax collector.
The Pharisee stood by himself and prayed this prayer:
'I thank you, God, that I am not a sinner like everyone
else. For I don't cheat, I don't sin, and I don't commit
adultery. I'm certainly not like that tax collector! I
fast twice a week, and I give you a tenth of my
income.' But the tax collector stood at a distance and
dared not even lift his eyes to Heaven as he prayed.
Instead, he beat his chest in sorrow, saying, 'O God,
be merciful to me, for I am a sinner.' I tell you this

sinner, not the Pharisee, returned home justified before God. For those who exalt themselves will be humbled, and those who humble themselves will be exalted." Luke 18:10-14

Jesus made it clear that it is never too late to change. He tells a parable in Matthew's Gospel about a man hiring workers to work in his field. He hires them throughout the day, even up to a few minutes before finish time. When finish time comes and he pays the men, he gives them all the same amount of money. Those who have worked all day complain that this is not fair, but the man hiring says:

"Friend, I haven't been unfair! Didn't you agree to work all day for the usual wage? Take your money and go. I wanted to pay this last worker the same as you. Is it against the law for me to do what I want with my money? Should you be jealous because I am kind to others?" Matthew 20: 13-15

This story shows us that there is no benefit to us if we compare our circumstances to others with jealousy; it makes us bitter and selfish. The workers who had been there all day would have been quite content if they'd not compared their earnings against what the later workers had been paid.

The hirer realised that all the workers needed the same pay to buy food for their families and paid them all according to their needs. The hirer represents God, who knows what we all need and offers it to us whether at the start of the day or at the finish. We have the choice of accepting or rejecting his offer.

Jesus was Clear What He Expected from His Followers, and Led by Example

As they were walking along, someone said to Jesus, "I will follow you wherever you go." But Jesus replied, "Foxes have dens to live in, and birds have nests, but the Son of Man has no place even to lay his head." He said to another person, "Come, follow me."

*The man agreed, but he said, "Lord, first let me
return home and bury my father." But Jesus told
him, "Let the spiritually dead bury their own dead!
Your duty is to go and preach about the Kingdom of
God." Another said, "Yes, Lord, I will follow you, but
first let me say good-bye to my family." But Jesus
told him, "Anyone who puts a hand to the plough and
then looks back is not fit for the Kingdom of God."
Luke 9:58-62*

Jesus was not being heartless here, but was emphasising the
importance of his message. He expected those who received the good
news to share it with others. He expects those who love and follow
him to obey his teaching:

*"Those who accept my commandments and obey
them are the ones who love me. And because they love
me, my Father will love them. And I will love them
and reveal myself to each of them." John 14:21*

And he emphasises how important it is to follow his
commandments: to love God and to love each other. Those who claim
to be Christian but don't love need to beware:

*"Not everyone who calls out to me, 'Lord! Lord!' will
enter the Kingdom of Heaven. Only those who
actually do the will of my Father in Heaven will
enter. On judgement day many will say to me, 'Lord!
Lord! We prophesied in your name and cast out
demons in your name and performed many miracles
in your name.' But I will reply, 'I never knew you.
Get away from me, you who break God's laws.'
Matthew 7: 21-23*

Jesus was able to look at everyone as an individual and
identify what that person needed:

*Once a religious leader asked Jesus this question,
"Good Teacher, what should I do to inherit eternal*

life?" "Why do you call me good?" Jesus asked him. "Only God is truly good. But to answer your question, you know the commandments: 'You must not commit adultery. You must not murder. You must not steal. You must not testify falsely. Honour your father and mother.'" The man replied, "I've obeyed all these commandments since I was young." When Jesus heard this answer, he said, "There is still one thing you haven't done. Sell all your possessions and give the money to the poor, and you will have treasure in Heaven. Then come, follow me." Luke 18: 18-22

This sounds very hard, but Jesus was telling the man that if he wanted to get right with God he would have to do much more than just following the laws. Jesus recognised that the man's money was the chain that was keeping him from eternal life: the man loved his money too much and he needed to love his fellow man. He needed to be free from his money so that he could follow God with all his heart. When the man was unable to do this, people asked who could meet such standards. Jesus replied:

"What is impossible for people is possible with God." Luke 18: 27

We cannot achieve perfection by our own strength, but if we allow him to God can make us perfect.

Jesus does not offer an easy life, but a life of love. Such a life can be hard; it took Jesus to the cross. But Jesus offers life in abundance:

"My purpose is to give them a rich and satisfying life." John 10:10

Jesus Lived and Taught the Paramount Importance of Love and Showed How to Love Others

The word love has become limited in use today. There is a tendency to think about love in the context of being in love, and of sexual love. Jesus doesn't teach about erotic love, but about caring love. It's hard to define such love, but I'll turn to the definition found in "The Road Less Travelled" by M Scott Peck, a professional counsellor. His definition of love is:

> *The will to extend one's self for the purpose of nurturing one's own or another's spiritual growth.*[141]

The first thing to note is that Jesus tells us to love everyone, not just our friends:

> *"Love your enemies! Do good to them. Lend to them without expecting to be repaid. Then your reward from Heaven will be very great, and you will truly be acting as children of the Most High, for he is kind to those who are unthankful and wicked." Luke 6:35*

> *"You have heard the law that says, 'Love your neighbour' and hate your enemy. But I say, love your enemies! Pray for those who persecute you! In that way, you will be acting as true children of your Father in Heaven. For he gives his sunlight to both the evil and the good, and he sends rain on the just and the unjust alike. If you love only those who love you, what reward is there for that? Even corrupt tax collectors do that much. If you are kind only to your friends, how are you different from anyone else? Even pagans do that. But you are to be perfect, even as your Father in Heaven is perfect." Matthew 5: 43-48*

Jesus demonstrated love in his dealings with everyone he met. He knew what each one needed in order to be free and he offered it to them—even the man who Jesus told to sell all of his possessions.

---

[141] *The Road Less Travelled: A New Psychology of Love, Traditional Values and Spiritual Growth* M Scott Peck ISBN 978-1846041075

The well-known parable of the Good Samaritan is a practical example of what it means to love others, even those you don't know:

> "A Jewish man was travelling from Jerusalem down to Jericho, and he was attacked by bandits. They stripped him of his clothes, beat him up, and left him half dead beside the road. By chance a priest came along. But when he saw the man lying there, he crossed to the other side of the road and passed him by. A temple assistant walked over and looked at him lying there, but he also passed by on the other side. Then a despised Samaritan came along, and when he saw the man, he felt compassion for him. Going over to him, the Samaritan soothed his wounds with olive oil and wine and bandaged them. Then he put the man on his own donkey and took him to an inn, where he took care of him. The next day he handed the innkeeper two silver coins, telling him, 'Take care of this man. If his bill runs higher than this, I'll pay you the next time I'm here.' Now which of these three would you say was a neighbour to the man who was attacked by bandits?" Jesus asked. The man replied, "The one who showed him mercy." Then Jesus said, "Yes, now go and do the same." Luke 10: 30-37

The most powerful demonstration of love is that Jesus allowed himself to be brutally killed because of his love for all of us. The Gospel of John tells us that:

> For God loved the world so much that he gave his one and only Son, so that everyone who believes in him will not perish but have eternal life. God sent his Son into the world not to judge the world, but to save the world through him. John 3: 16-17

The Jewish law said that a sin could be forgiven by offering a sacrifice, killing an innocent animal that took on a person's sin and carried it from them — the sacrificial animal was punished for the sin

213

and justice was satisfied. Speaking in the religious language of his day, Jesus made himself the sacrifice. He carried the peoples' sin, and took the punishment that they (and we) deserve for sin. If they (and we) accept his sacrifice then we will not be punished as we deserve; we can be free from our past. But to accept the sacrifice we have to admit that we have been sinful, to regret it, and to want to live a life of love in the future. The self-sacrifice that Jesus made is the most extreme form of "extending one's self for the purpose of nurturing one's own or another's spiritual growth" and is the same love that Jesus expects of his followers:

> "This is my commandment: Love each other in the same way I have loved you. There is no greater love than to lay down one's life for one's friends. You are my friends if you do what I command." John 15: 13-14

Jesus Lived and Taught About Forgiveness, and not Judging Others

Jesus tells us not to judge others, and in the same way we will not be judged, and he tells us to forgive others, and in the same way we will be forgiven. This is a message at the centre of the Lord's Prayer *"forgive us our sins, as we forgive those who sin against us."* We find that not only did Jesus teach this, he lived it. Right at the end, when he was nailed on the cross and dying he called out *"Father, forgive them."*

He taught that we should never stop forgiving others:

> Then Peter came to him and asked, "Lord, how often should I forgive someone who sins against me? Seven times?" "No, not seven times," Jesus replied, "but seventy times seven!" Matthew 18: 21-22

Jesus is saying that we can expect God to treat us like we treat others. Jesus hated hypocrisy and so we can trust that he will treat us in the same way that he tells us to treat others. If we ask his forgiveness, it will be given.

He also understood how we judge others but try to justify ourselves. He advised against this sort of hypocrisy:

> *"Do not judge others, and you will not be judged. For you will be treated as you treat others. The standard you use in judging is the standard by which you will be judged. And why worry about a speck in your friend's eye when you have a log in your own? How can you think of saying to your friend, 'Let me help you get rid of that speck in your eye,' when you can't see past the log in your own eye? Hypocrite! First get rid of the log in your own eye; then you will see well enough to deal with the speck in your friend's eye."* Matthew 7:1-5

Consider also the story of the woman caught in adultery:

> *The teachers of religious law and the Pharisees brought a woman who had been caught in the act of adultery. They put her in front of the crowd. "Teacher," they said to Jesus, "this woman was caught in the act of adultery. The Law of Moses says to stone her. What do you say?" They were trying to trap him into saying something they could use against him, but Jesus stooped down and wrote in the dust with his finger. They kept demanding an answer, so he stood up again and said, "All right, but let the one who has never sinned throw the first stone!" Then he stooped down again and wrote in the dust. When the accusers heard this, they slipped away one by one, beginning with the oldest, until only Jesus was left in the middle of the crowd with the woman. Then Jesus stood up again and said to the woman, "Where are your accusers? Didn't even one of them condemn you?" "No, Lord," she said. And Jesus said, "Neither do I. Go and sin no more." John 8: 3-11*

Not even Jesus condemned the woman—so we can all hope for forgiveness for our sins. But he did say, *"Go and sin no more."*

Jesus Lived and Taught How to Relate to God

The Jewish people were in no doubt that there was a God. Jesus' teaching recognised this. He knew that those he was speaking to would pray, and he advised honesty and humility. He described how the goal was to relate to God, and not to show off to anyone who might be watching:

> *"When you pray, don't be like the hypocrites who love to pray publicly on street corners and in the synagogues where everyone can see them. I tell you the truth. That is all the reward they will ever get. But when you pray, go away by yourself, shut the door behind you, and pray to your Father in private. Then your Father, who sees everything, will reward you. When you pray, don't babble on and on as people of other religions do. They think their prayers are answered merely by repeating their words again and again. Don't be like them, for your Father knows exactly what you need even before you ask him!"*
> *Matthew 6:5-8*

In Conclusion

The Gospel accounts contain deep wisdom about how to view ourselves, our neighbours and God. We learn the power of forgiveness, for ourselves and for others. We learn what true love is. We learn what true leadership is. We learn what is important and unimportant in our heart. We find a path to freedom and to honourable righteousness, and we learn that we have the chance to take that path without fear of condemnation.

There are many other books which contain wisdom about life, yet the New Testament documents describe more than just wise words. They describe miracles. We might understand some as incredible co-incidences (such as telling an expert fisherman exactly where to catch a net full of fish, after he's been fishing unsuccessfully all night). Others we might understand as clever psychotherapy (healing a man from demons) or exercising hypnotic or similar healing powers (healing a man from leprosy, giving sight to the blind); using the power of the mind to heal the body. But others are more difficult to rationalise away (bringing Lazarus back from the dead after several days buried in a tomb, walking on water, turning water into wine, controlling the weather).

And the New Testament documents describe one particularly special and outrageous event. They describe that Jesus of Nazareth came back to life two days after being brutally whipped and crucified, and having a spear thrust in his side. The documents record eyewitnesses attesting this, sometimes forfeiting their lives on account of their testimony. The facts are corroborated by independent sources outside of the community of Jesus' followers. The gospels describe how Jesus appeared in a solid bodily form to his followers; they could touch him and he could eat real food. One thing is clear: the writers had complete conviction that God exists, and that Jesus of Nazareth was "the Messiah."

Jesus performed miracles and healing, but that was not why he came. His miracles and healings were his credentials They showed that he was one who speaks with the authority of God, and one who loves people so much that he sacrificed his life for us. He said that "*if you have seen me you have seen the father,*" so when Jesus instructs, it is wise to listen.

Central to what Jesus taught was that our purpose is to love: love God and love each other. Jesus was adamant that religious ritual and rules must not be allowed to interfere with that love—rituals are in themselves worthless.

And finally Jesus demonstrated that the death of our bodies is not the death of us; we are spiritual beings that outlast our present physical bodies.

Chapter 8: The Way of the Minimalist Christian

As promised in the introduction, this book has explored a number of conclusions.

- Everyone relies on faith.
- Science describes an incredible universe.
- The universe exhibits design and purpose.
- Not everything can be explained by science.
- Reason leads to a sound definition of God.
- Jesus lived and spoke for God.
- God has a purpose for each of us.

This chapter describes what it might look like to live in the light of those conclusions, in what I call "The Way of the Minimalist Christian."

Who Do We Want to Be?

People with clear goals get a lot closer to achieving them than those who don't! However, we may look at goal-driven people and conclude that we don't like their goals. The UK TV program *The Apprentice* follows a group of self-driven, self-centred ambitious young men and women as they compete to become Sir Alan Sugar's apprentice; a job with a "five figure salary." I enjoy the show but I simply wouldn't want to behave like that.

Whilst it is motivating to strive for a goal, it is important that we have the right goal: the right vision and purpose for our lives. For me, Jesus Christ provides that vision and that purpose; he demonstrated it in his own life. Jesus was the perfect man. In his attitude, what he said and did, and in how he loved he demonstrated what it means to fully reach our potential.

- He demonstrated extreme love and selflessness throughout and up to the end of his life
- He saw each individual as someone of value. He had time for everyone

- He was not afraid to tell people what they really needed to hear
- He had that supreme confidence that comes from knowing that he was truly loved by God

Clearly, nobody can force us to become like that. Nobody can force us to build a selfless, forgiving, loving heart; we have to choose it for ourselves. We have to want to change in order to be able to change. An angry parent telling a child, "You should be more like him" will be far less effective than the child deciding for himself "I want to be more like him."

How do we find out where our heart lies? Imagine your own funeral. The man at the front is describing your character. Which of the following two lists of words would you hope to find him using: the left-hand list or the right-hand list? Or imagine that you are at a Christening. Would you want to see the innocent baby grow up as described in the left-hand list or the right-hand list?

Selfless	Self-centred
Courageous	Cowardly
Forgiving	Judgemental
Having Integrity	Hypocrite
Hard working	Lazy
Generous	Greedy
Honest	Swindler
Peaceful	Violent
Loving	Indifferent

The attributes on the left are the attributes of a healthy individual and a healthy society. These attributes were demonstrated by Jesus Christ. So let's take that as the vision of our true self. That is how we want to be described in our obituary, but it is not where we are today. Today we may find that some of the attributes in the right-hand column could apply to us, and probably we don't like ourselves for being like that. We need to do something about it. We need to grasp the vision of who we want to be and focus on becoming that person. How do we do that?

According to Jesus, the first thing is to repent of our past and receive forgiveness. Repenting is not an easy word, and is not in common usage anymore (except in church circles). It is how we respond when we recognise that we are not who we are meant to be; when we recognise that we are becoming a person described on right-hand list above. Simply speaking, repentance is admitting that, "I don't want to be the self-centred cowardly judgemental hypocritical lazy greedy swindling violent person that I am today. I want to be selfless and loving to others; a left-list person. I'm sorry about all of those things that I've said and done which have hurt others and I wish they hadn't happened, but they did and I can't do anything about them now. But I don't want to be like that in the future."

But who can forgive us of our past? If we reach the position of really wanting to change, then we will probably find that we are our own toughest judge. Often, we feel that we can only forgive ourselves if we know that we have truly been forgiven by the one we hurt in the first place, and that justice has been done.

Jesus was extremely clear that he had the authority to forgive sins, and continues to have that authority today. In Anselm's language, when we have chosen to do something wrong, we have done it through Evil, the opposite of Goodness. So God, who is Goodness, can forgive us on behalf of the person who we have hurt. Goodness requires that they forgive us, and so if they were to choose not to, then their un-forgiveness would be done through Evil. So God's goodness forgives those who repent.

Minimalist Christianity

When I was a child, I wasn't taught about God. I did have RE (Religious Education), which told me lots of "unbelievable" stories—men being swallowed by whales for instance. These strengthened my developing idea that religion was just a delusion that simple people needed to help them cope in difficult circumstances. At about the age of 14, I "knew" that science had disproved God, and that the idea of worshiping something supernatural was outdated. I was so confident that all religion was rubbish that I stopped entering into serious discussion with Christians. I knew that I could disprove their ideas, but since they must need the emotional crutch I didn't want to take that away from them. So for over twenty years I never had a serious discussion about God, my life was generally fine and comfortable and I had no need or desire to find out about God.

There was a very difficult time when my father was dying of prostate cancer, and another when my wife and I lost our first child who died at birth. I wept, but dealt with them myself—and with the help of my wife. I didn't have or know any God to help me. I didn't miss him.

But I came to change my mind.

I made the mistake of joining in a discussion around our kitchen table about why people weren't attracted to church, and I started to explain why not. They listened, but my open-mindedness was challenged. I was challenged to wonder why otherwise sane people seemed happy to believe in a God. I decided to explore whether there was actually any sense behind Christianity. And to do that properly I had to at least accept that there was a possibility that it might be correct, rather than just trying to pick holes in it.

I had to admit that I didn't really know what Christianity was. I'd only seen the cringy outside view: the street preacher telling me I was going to Hell, the *Songs of Praise* slot on TV, the open sandals and tambourines. So I started as best I could to find out if there was anything behind the awful image, and the friend from the discussion leant me a book, *Beyond Belief*[142] which gave me an introduction to Christianity.

---

[142] *Beyond Belief* Peter Meadows & Joseph Steinberg with Donna Vann ISBN 1 86024 321 5

I think it's fair to say that the man Jesus touched my heart. Someone who goes to the trouble of allowing himself to be nailed to a cross at least deserves a hearing, and I found that he came across as a pretty decent chap. I began to wonder why today everyone seemed to dislike him. Perhaps it was as Ghandi said "I like your Christ, I don't like your Christians." So there began an attraction to Jesus, but I needed to know whether there was any factual basis too. I was surprised to find that there was a lot of archaeological corroboration for what was written in the Bible, and I came across a reasonable scientific explanation for the plagues of Egypt. I found it impossible to doubt that Jesus tomb was empty a few days after he was crucified, and it seemed clear that neither side could have taken the body—it just didn't match their behaviour or subsequent events.[143] I came from a background of "miracles don't happen" and so this was quite a challenge. But I began to realise that if God created everything then he could do what he liked.

Eventually in the journal that I was keeping I wrote the question: "So what have I decided?" It was time to get off the fence! I wrote that I would "give God a chance." And at that moment I felt an overwhelming experience of joy and release. For forty years I had built a consistent worldview from the atheist/agnostic side of the fence, and since that moment I have built a consistent worldview from the Christian side of the fence. Both outlooks are intellectually possible and consistent, but at the end of the day my heart knows and my mind sees that there is a creator, and that Jesus is central to our understanding of our purpose in the universe. I write this book, not to win arguments, but to give others the opportunity to have the same experience that I've had.

And part of that experience is that there is an awful lot of baggage, dogmatism, and judgementalism amongst many outspoken people who claim to be Christians. I am embarrassed by much of the behaviour of so-called Christians, but I also am in admiration of many true Christians.

---

[143] *Who Moved the Stone* Frank Morison ISBN 978-1850786740

I find that Christ had a very simple message, one that speaks truth and speaks to the heart, but that over the centuries we have cluttered it up with our own opinions and interpretations, unwilling to compromise or agree and dogmatic in our opinions.

I long for a world where we all adopt the simple message again, where we can all believe and we can all become who we are meant to be. I call that Minimalist Christianity.

In the following passage taken from *The Barbarian Way*, Erwin Raphael McManus gives a flavour of what that means:

> *Strangely enough though, some who come to Jesus Christ seem to immediately and fully embrace this barbarian way. They live their lives with every step moving forward and with every fibre of their being fighting for the heart of their King. Jesus Christ has become the all-consuming passion of their lives. They are not about religion or position. They have little patience for institutions or bureaucracies. Their lack of respect for tradition or ritual makes them uncivilised to those who love religion. When asked if they are Christians, their answer might surprisingly be no, they are passionate followers of Jesus Christ. They see Christianity as a world religion, in many ways no different from any other religious system. Whether Buddhism, Hinduism, Islam, or Christianity, they're not about religion; they're about advancing the revolution Jesus started two thousand years ago.*[144]

The simplest explanation of the life of a Minimalist Christian is someone who does their utmost to love God and their fellow man, and to follow Jesus' teaching. There is no formula, or set of rules to follow, it is more a case of striving for a Christ-like character or heart:

---

[144] *The Barbarian Way* Erwin Raphael McManus ISBN 978-0-7852-6432-3

It seems to be in our nature to want rules. We want to be told what we can do and what we can't do. We don't want to have to think. Take driving for example. We know that we shouldn't go at high speed in built up areas, so why do we need to be told that we mustn't go above 30 miles per hour? What's special about 30, why not 29, or 33?

Setting a rule is a way of avoiding guilt. We prefer to pretend that we are not guilty rather than that accept we are guilty and ask for forgiveness. If I go at 29 miles per hour and knock someone over, then you can't accuse me of going too fast—I was within the speed limit. I can say "it wasn't my fault—it was the person who set the speed limit."

This is living the Old Testament way: "Thou shalt not exceed 30 miles per hour in a built up zone."

If we were to ask Jesus then he would say "Don't go so fast that you knock someone over." It's a much tougher requirement, and means that there is no way we can escape our personal responsibility. If we knock someone over it's our fault and that's that. All we can do is to ask for forgiveness, to which he would reply "Are you really sorry? Are you going to change your driving habits so that you don't do it again? Yes? Then I forgive you."

Tougher, isn't it? I have to take full responsibility, and I have to be humble enough to admit that I was wrong and to ask for forgiveness.

Christians, as anyone else would, find it difficult trying to live a life which is totally without laws, but where the standard is perfection. There is no speed limit, but you are responsible if your driving harms someone. So we make up our own laws. Some are moral, some are conventions or traditions. Although

Christianity is about freedom, we have tied ourselves up in chains again.

Everybody does it without realising it. Have you ever been to a conference or meeting that runs over a couple of days? On day one, we look round the room and then choose a seat. Next day, that's our seat — we go straight there. It's easiest, it worked yesterday, but we've just made up a little law: "that's where I sit." It's OK to make up rules, so long as we don't let the rule become more important than the issue it's solving. We need to keep remembering the reason behind the law. Going 30 miles an hour in itself is not important; avoiding running someone over is the issue. Christians need to be wary of our natural love of rules and laws. Jesus looks at the heart; do we want to do what is right or do we want just to keep the law?[145]

This attitude is central to our approach to life and we use the teaching of Jesus as a guide to what this might look like in our day-to-day actions. Christian literature offers advice on what Christian life looks like, but it is essential to go right back to the source: the record of Jesus' teaching in the gospels, and in particular the Sermon on the Mount.

What Are We to Make of the Bible?

The Bible is of course central to Christian teaching, but sometimes it is taken to be the *only* source of knowledge about God. For some, the choice between believing something written in the Bible and a scientifically-verified fact is to choose the Bible. Why? Because they have been told that it is the inerrant word of God and cannot be questioned.

---

[145] *The Leap* Phil Hemsley ISBN 978-1-4389-2935-4

The book of Revelation ends with the words:

And I solemnly declare to everyone who hears the words of prophecy written in this book: If anyone adds anything to what is written here, God will add to that person the plagues described in this book. And if anyone removes any of the words from this book of prophecy, God will remove that person's share in the tree of life and in the holy city that are described in this book. Revelation 22: 18-19

That's seriously scary stuff. For one who believes in God as the entity or being who created us and everything around us, a threat in the holy book of God is something to be taken seriously. But the Bible is not God, and it seems to me that often Christians choose to worship the Bible rather than God. And that leads to problems because the Bible was written by humans, and is routinely translated into many different languages and using many different styles by humans. Such is the fear of mistranslation that some Christians will only use the King James Version, claiming that all others are flawed. This view of the Bible influences Christian behaviour. I recently read a prayer that a congregation was being asked to pray:

Lord, from this day forward, I will accept the Bible as your flawless Word to me and I will make it the Final Authority for my life—even when I don't understand it, it is not popular, it is not easy, or I don't like it. You are God and I am not. Thank you for loving me enough to speak to me through your Word. Amen.

Yes, God is God and we are not, but the Bible is not God either and to pretend that it is the perfect, complete and only valid communication that God intends to have with humanity seems to me to be extremely wrong and extremely dangerous. I don't view the Bible in that way, and I am not alone. The following is taken from an on-line Bible study course. I find the last sentence very important.

There are four reasons why claims that the Bible is literally the infallible or inerrant word of God are

226

misleading. First, the Bible has a history and because of that history Roman Catholic and Protestant Bibles are not the same. How are we to decide which Bible is infallible or inerrant? Second, in English we read the Bible in translation and there are many human choices made in the process of reconciling ancient manuscripts and interpreting the meaning of Hebrew and Greek texts. If there is no original manuscript of the Bible available to us, what does it mean to claim that the Bible is literally the word of God? Third, confessions in the Reformed tradition of Christian faith do not simply support the view that the Bible is literally the infallible or inerrant word of God. These confessions clearly affirm the authority of the Bible but acknowledge the need for interpretation. And fourth, arguments in theology for the infallibility or inerrancy of the Bible were developed after the Reformation to resist Catholic claims of infallible teaching authority and also methods for historical and literary analysis of the Bible. The Bible does not present itself as infallible or inerrant, but Christians have made these claims in order to advance their own interpretations of scripture.[146]

Don't misunderstand me, I strongly believe that the Bible is an excellent book and that we learn a great deal about God and about ourselves through the Bible, but we must not confine God to the pages of a book and we must not worship a book rather than God. Christians who view the Bible as inerrant have to develop theologies that accommodate every phrase in the Bible, as if it were an instruction manual. It satisfies our craving for rules, but it misses the message of the heart and ignores the provenance of the Bible itself.

---

[146] http://christian-bible.com/Exegesis/inerrancy.htm accessed 10/6/13

In practice, it is hard for Christians to define what the Bible is, and how to interpret it, particularly the Old Testament. It contains different documents that serve different purposes. Perhaps the best thing is to investigate sufficiently to draw one's own conclusions.

The Old Testament

There is no doubt that overall the Bible is a daunting book of typically 1000 pages. The biggest proportion of the text is the Old Testament, and Christian teaching today spends a lot of time on passages from the Old Testament. As mentioned above, some Christians view the Bible is the inerrant word of God. If nothing else this raises difficulties when it comes to the many descriptions of murder, rape, massacre and other "unpleasant" behaviour by many of the characters in the Old Testament. Does this mean that God advocates or even instructs this sort of behaviour? Or if these passages are simply descriptions of what happened, then in what way are they the inerrant word of God? And of course there is the book of Genesis which describes the creation of the world, the stars and planets, the plants and animals, man and woman. It is troublesome because, as we have discussed before, there are some who insist that it is a literal description of the mechanism whereby the world /universe came into being, and some advocate that the world is only 6000 years old, based on the recorded lineage from Adam to Jesus.

To my mind it is better to think of the Old Testament as pre-Christian literature, which helps explain the belief system of people in Israel at the time of Jesus.

The first five books, Genesis, Exodus, Leviticus, Numbers and Deuteronomy are referred to as the Pentateuch. The word Pentateuch means "five vessels," "five containers," or "five-volume book."

Genesis starts with a story of the creation of the universe, plants and animals, and of mankind through the creation of Adam. It describes that when God created human beings he made them "in his image" and that once God and Adam would walk together in the Garden of Eden, but that Adam and Eve ate the forbidden fruit of the tree of the knowledge of good and evil and so were thrown out of the garden. The passage conveys that God created and upholds everything, and that like God we know right and wrong.

The book of Genesis then continues with what is basically the beginning of the history of the Jewish people. It describes the lives of many of the ancient characters, Noah, Abraham, Isaac, Jacob and Joseph. It explains why the people of Israel (another name for Jacob) came to be in Egypt. The history continues through Exodus, when the Israelites leave slavery in Egypt under Moses. Exodus contains the laws of the Israelite nation, the Ten Commandments, the regulations on how to worship, different offerings and sacrifices to be made, rules of behaviour and social responsibilities.

The story of the Israelite nation under Moses continues through Leviticus, Numbers, and Deuteronomy, at which point Moses dies.

The next twelve books are referred to as the Historical Books.

Joshua was the leader who followed Moses, and the book bearing his name describes how the Israelites conquered and inhabited the "Promised Land."

The history continues through Judges. The Israelites did not at this time have a king, but were led by "judges." It's not particularly clear what the difference was between a judge and a king, but the book describes the many judges and how Israel fared under their leadership.

The short book of Ruth describes the personal story of a woman, Ruth, trying to act for the best in difficult times.

The books of Samuel continue the history further. The prophet Samuel crowns Saul the first king of Israel, and later crowns David to be his successor.

The books of Kings continue the history after David, listing all of the subsequent kings of Israel along with the main events of their reigns. Much of the history is repeated through Chronicles, but with additional details added such as the measurements of buildings, the names of people in key jobs, the numbers of people in different tribes and the sizes of armies. At the end of Chronicles, the Israelite nation has been captured and exiled to Babylon.

The books of Ezra, Nehemiah and Esther describe the return to Israel, and the part played by those whose names are on the books.

Up to this point the Old Testament is largely the history of the Jewish people, including description of their interaction with their God. Often individuals are described as representing God speaking to the nation. The success or failure in war, and the prosperity is often related according to whether the leader acts well or badly in the eyes of God. The books contain descriptions of very human acts of great bravery, stupidity, cowardice, selfishness, love, revenge and many other attributes.

The next five books (Job, Psalms, Proverbs, Ecclesiastes, The Song of Solomon) are referred to as Poetical Books, and I'll dwell a little more on these as I rather like the timeless wisdom in them:

Early in the book of Job we read that

> One day the members of the heavenly court came to present themselves before the Lord, and the Accuser, Satan came with them. "Where have you come from?" the Lord asked Satan. Satan answered the Lord, "I have been patrolling the earth, watching everything that's going on." Then the Lord asked Satan, "Have you noticed my servant Job? He is the finest man in all the earth. He is blameless—a man of complete integrity. He fears God and stays away from evil."

> Satan replied to the Lord, "Yes, but Job has good reason to fear God. You have always put a wall of protection around him and his home and his property. You have made him prosper in everything he does. Look how rich he is! But reach out and take

away everything he has, and he will surely curse you to your face!"

"All right, you may test him," the Lord said to Satan. "Do whatever you want with everything he possesses, but don't harm him physically." So Satan left the Lord's presence. Job 1: 6-12

And the book goes on to describe awful calamities befalling Job, and four friends coming to try to persuade him that it's all happened because he's been sinful. Finally God comes and points out that he can do what he likes, and is not bounded by human constraints. In the end Job is greatly rewarded for his integrity.

I personally doubt that the book of Job describes real events, but I think it is included to teach important aspects about the relationship between man and God.

The book of Psalms is a book of songs or poems to God, many written by King David.

The book of Proverbs is a collection of wise sayings written by King Solomon, who is also thought to have written *Ecclesiastes*, an essay on the futility of life. Here is a sample:

These are the words of the Teacher, King David's son, who ruled in Jerusalem.

"Everything is meaningless," says the Teacher, "completely meaningless!" What do people get for all their hard work under the sun? Generations come and generations go, but the earth never changes. The sun rises and the sun sets, then hurries around to rise again. The wind blows south, and then turns north. Around and around it goes, blowing in circles. Rivers run into the sea, but the sea is never full. Then the water returns again to the rivers and flows out again to the sea. Everything is wearisome beyond description. No matter how much we see, we are never satisfied. No matter how much we hear, we are

not content. History merely repeats itself. It has all been done before. Nothing under the sun is truly new. Sometimes people say, "Here is something new!" But actually it is old; nothing is ever truly new. We don't remember what happened in the past, and in future generations, no one will remember what we are doing now. Ecclesiastes 1: 1-9

And it finishes with advice to "remember your creator" and:

Here now is my final conclusion: Fear God and obey his commands, for this is everyone's duty. God will judge us for everything we do, including every secret thing, whether good or bad. Ecclesiastes 12: 13-14

The final Poetical Book is Solomon's Song of Songs. This is a bizarre book, quite unlike what I expected to find in the Bible. It is a very intimate poem between two lovers, a young woman and a young man. Here is just a small taste of the poem:

You have captured my heart, my treasure, my bride.

You hold it hostage with one glance of your eyes, with a single jewel of your necklace.

Your love delights me, my treasure, my bride.

Your love is better than wine, your perfume more fragrant than spices.

Your lips are as sweet as nectar, my bride.

Honey and milk are under your tongue. Your clothes are scented like the cedars of Lebanon.

You are my private garden, my treasure, my bride, a secluded spring, a hidden fountain.

Your thighs shelter a paradise of pomegranates with rare spices — henna with nard, nard and saffron, fragrant calamus and cinnamon, with all the trees of frankincense, myrrh, and aloes, and every other lovely spice.

You are a garden fountain, a well of fresh water streaming down from Lebanon's mountains.

Song of Songs 4: 9-15

The remaining books in the Old Testament are labelled Prophetical, with five Major Prophets and twelve Minor Prophets; the terms Major and Minor refer to the length of the books rather than the significance or stature of the prophets.

These books record what "the sovereign Lord" or "the Lord of Heaven's armies" says about various issues, often the disobedience, depravity or basic nastiness of the Israelites. They record prophetic visions, foretelling events in the future. There are entreaties from God to the Israelites to be good and to be faithful, and explanations of why they are suffering discomfort and what they are doing which is not pleasing to God. The messages are sometimes very simple:

> *O people, the Lord has told you what is good, and this is what he requires of you: to do what is right, to love mercy, and to walk humbly with your God. Micah 6: 8*

And sometimes it seems that God is tired of the rituals and "religion" of the Israelites:

> *And so the Lord says, "These people say they are mine. They honour me with their lips, but their hearts are far from me. And their worship of me is nothing but man-made rules learned by rote." Isaiah 29: 13*

However, there are also many references to the coming of a future saviour or king. Here for example from Isaiah:

> *Out of the stump of David's family will grow a shoot, yes, a new Branch bearing fruit from the old root.*

And the Spirit of the Lord will rest on him, the Spirit of wisdom and understanding, the Spirit of counsel and might, the Spirit of knowledge and the fear of the Lord. He will delight in obeying the Lord. He will not judge by appearance nor make a decision based on hearsay. He will give justice to the poor and make fair decisions for the exploited. The earth will shake at the force of his word, and one breath from his mouth will destroy the wicked. He will wear righteousness like a belt and truth like an undergarment. Isaiah 11: 1-8

And here's another very important prophetic passage from Isaiah. This is generally taken to point to Jesus, and in particular to explain the central message of Christianity, that through Jesus' death on the cross we have all been made right with God and that when we repent our sins have already been forgiven:

My servant grew up in the Lord's presence like a tender green shoot, like a root in dry ground. There was nothing beautiful or majestic about his appearance, nothing to attract us to him. He was despised and rejected, a man of sorrows, acquainted with deepest grief.

We turned our backs on him and looked the other way. He was despised, and we did not care.

Yet it was our weaknesses he carried; it was our sorrows that weighed him down. And we thought his troubles were a punishment from God, a punishment for his own sins!

But he was pierced for our rebellion, crushed for our sins.

He was beaten so we could be whole.

He was whipped so we could be healed.

All of us, like sheep, have strayed away. We have left God's paths to follow our own. Yet the Lord laid on him the sins of us all.

He was oppressed and treated harshly, yet he never said a word. He was led like a lamb to the slaughter. And as a sheep is silent before the shearers, he did not open his mouth. Unjustly condemned, he was led away. No one cared that he died without descendants, that his life was cut short in midstream. But he was struck down for the rebellion of my people.

He had done no wrong and had never deceived anyone. But he was buried like a criminal; he was put in a rich man's grave.

But it was the Lord's good plan to crush him and cause him grief. Yet when his life is made an offering for sin, he will have many descendants. He will enjoy a long life, and the Lord's good plan will prosper in his hands. When he sees all that is accomplished by his anguish, he will be satisfied. And because of his experience, my righteous servant will make it possible for many to be counted righteous, for he will bear all their sins.

I will give him the honours of a victorious soldier, because he exposed himself to death. He was counted among the rebels. He bore the sins of many and interceded for rebels. Isaiah 53:2-12

This reference is taken from Micah:

But you, O Bethlehem Ephrathah, are only a small village among all the people of Judah. Yet a ruler of Israel will come from you, one whose origins are from the distant past. The people of Israel will be abandoned to their enemies until the woman in labour gives birth. Then at last his fellow

235

countrymen will return from exile to their own land. And he will stand to lead his flock with the Lord's strength, in the majesty of the name of the Lord his God. Then his people will live there undisturbed, for he will be highly honoured around the world. And he will be the source of peace. Micah 5:2-5

These all describe events in Jesus' life in surprisingly close detail, in particular his death and his birth and parental line—all as recorded in the New Testament documents.

So what is the Old Testament? It is a historical record of the Jewish nation, it contains wise saying and essays, it has inspirational stories, it teaches love and romance, and it makes various prophecies and perhaps one of the most important aspects is that it has some very precise passages foretelling the coming of Jesus.

The Old Testament contains the Ten Commandments, along with other quite detailed laws. Many of these are sound moral and ethical principles, but some of the detailed laws are only specific to the people at the time (the wearing of clothes with tassels for instance). It is not always clear what is poetry or parable and what is historical fact, and it would be very dangerous to take it as an instruction manual for life, and in particular it should not be taken as a rule book by which to judge others.

If we read the New Testament carefully it tells us that much of what is recorded in the historical passages in the Old Testament is not at all pleasing to God! As such, the Old Testament is not central to Minimalist Christianity.

Sometimes We Need to Stop Sitting on the Fence.

It may be that for most of our lives we don't even think about Jesus Christ, but when we do there comes a time when sitting on the fence is no longer an option.

We all want to live a "good life," but we struggle to know what it is. One of the attractions of Jesus' teaching is that it rekindles that desire in us and it helps us to understand what a "good life" looks like. His teaching affirms what we feel in our hearts, and paints a more extreme goodness than we can imagine in a world where we are assailed by messages that preach self-centredness and expectation of perfection in others. But perhaps the most liberating instructions he gives concern judgement and forgiveness. We are not to judge others but show mercy, and we are to forgive and know that to can be forgiven. How much better the world would be if we could all accept these two pillars.

Perhaps the biggest problem that we have today is that we have forgotten or cannot embrace the awe that is God. We are dazzled by pretty technology, our iPads, our 3D TVs, and we have lost the sense of awe that we find in the men and women in the Bible. We can't conjure up feelings of God's awesome power just by singing songs in churches about "How great you are," or how "Our God reigns" when we don't recognise God's hand in the things that surround us.

That's why we need to look again at all that science shows us about the universe. The universe is God's design—it's amazing and it points to an amazing God. We need to rekindle respect for the creator and sustainer of the universe. Then we will be fearful of putting words into his mouth, of criticising other people, and of taking liberties with his creation. We need to be able to hold him in the proper reverence once more.

And so Minimalist Christianity embraces all the scientific discoveries that have been made, the wisdom and healing described in the New Testament documents, and the corresponding existence of God. We don't need to dogmatically claim scientific fact in the Creation narrative. Instead we can interpret scientific discovery as an exploration and unveiling of the wonders of Creation.

We can marvel at the universe, the galaxies, the stars, the balance of powerful forces and unimaginable distances.

We can wonder at the "weird" behaviour of the subatomic particles, and speculate whether everything really only comes into existence when we observe it.

We can look with incredulity at the fantastic complexity that is life and particularly mankind today, and the amazing processes that have been gone through to reach the present point in time.

We can feel stunned admiration at the love and courage shown by Jesus Christ during his life, and in willingly submitting to crucifixion.

And we can give praise where praise is due; to the God who masterminded it all, created it all, sustains it all and is intimately involved in his Creation.

But how do we relate to such a God? A good response is choosing to live according to the will of Jesus Christ, knowing that we are loved and forgiven by God, and accepting the freedom that that brings.

The next thing is prayer.

> "When you pray, don't be like the hypocrites who love to pray publicly on street corners and in the synagogues where everyone can see them. I tell you the truth, that is all the reward they will ever get. But when you pray, go away by yourself, shut the door behind you, and pray to your Father in private. Then your Father, who sees everything, will reward you.
>
> When you pray, don't babble on and on as people of other religions do. They think their prayers are answered merely by repeating their words again and again. Don't be like them, for your Father knows exactly what you need even before you ask him! Pray like this:
>
> Our Father in Heaven, may your name be kept holy.
>
> May your Kingdom come soon.

May your will be done on earth, as it is in Heaven.

Give us today the food we need, and forgive us our sins, as we have forgiven those who sin against us.

And don't let us yield to temptation, but rescue us from the evil one."

Matthew 6: 5-14

We all know that we have lived self-centred and selfish lives that are not as God intended. God knows that, and he graciously gives us the chance to change how we live. It was the same immediately after Jesus' crucifixion. People asked his disciple Peter what they had to do:

Peter's words pierced their hearts, and they said to him and to the other apostles, "Brothers, what should we do?" Peter replied, "Each of you must repent of your sins and turn to God, and be baptised in the name of Jesus Christ for the forgiveness of your sins. Then you will receive the gift of the Holy Spirit. This promise is to you, and to your children, and even to people far in the future—all who have been called by the Lord our God." Then Peter continued preaching for a long time, strongly urging all his listeners, "Save yourselves from this crooked generation!" Acts 2:37

Both of these require humility. Praying and repenting mean that we are admitting that God is greater than we are, and that we are taking responsibility for things we've done wrong, submitting to his will and asking for forgiveness. They are tough things to do, but there can be great release when we finally admit that we are not the centre of the universe. We are released to begin to be the sort of person that we'd like to be. We are forgiven our past and free to move on. We can begin to live as God intended.

I can't promise that it is easy. Changing beliefs, changing habits, choosing to submit and choosing to be open about our shortcomings are not easy things to do. So take encouragement where you can. Often passages in the Bible can be encouraging, like in Paul's letter to the Hebrews:

Therefore, since we are surrounded by such a huge crowd of witnesses to the life of faith, let us strip off every weight that slows us down, especially the sin that so easily trips us up. And let us run with endurance the race God has set before us. We do this by keeping our eyes on Jesus, the champion who initiates and perfects our faith. Because of the joy awaiting him, he endured the cross, disregarding its shame. Now he is seated in the place of honour beside God's throne. Think of all the hostility he endured from sinful people; then you won't become weary and give up. After all, you have not yet given your lives in your struggle against sin. Hebrews 12:1-4

Before I chose to become a Christian I was surprised by someone who said, "Why don't you just try it?" I don't think that we can adopt a belief system without having thought about it and explored it first. But perhaps having reached the end of this book you may be at the point of saying "Maybe this is for me." I hope that what you have read has allowed you to consider with an open mind, and I also hope that you find a resonance between Minimalist Christianity and what your heart tells you about how you want to live.

My final suggestion is that if you find the idea of following Christ attractive then make a decision. I described how I decided "to give God a chance." All that I will say is that he took it!

Appendix 1: Common Logical Fallacies

Straw Man

The person using the straw man fallacy argues a case by presenting a false and often simplified version of the opponent's argument and then easily knocks it down. This fallacy can be surprisingly common particularly in discussions about the existence or otherwise of God.

Slippery Slope

The "slippery slope" fallacy implies that an action will lead to a sequence of events ending in disaster, and that therefore the action mustn't me taken.

For example: "If you believe in God you might become a religious fundamentalist. Religious fundamentalists flew into the twin towers so you shouldn't believe in God."

Ad Populum

This is an appeal to our basic desire to fit in with the crowd. I have seen heated discussions about how many scientists believe in God. The answer is of no relevance to the question of whether God exists or not. The reason behind the numbers might be relevant, but the numbers themselves are of no consequence.

The Fallacy Fallacy

A logical fallacy is a mistake in reasoning, but to commit a logical fallacy doesn't mean that the case being argued is incorrect. The facts being argued may be correct but the case is being made with poor reasoning.

Missing the Point

When evidence implies a conclusion, but the conclusion that is drawn is not the correct conclusion, or is extrapolating beyond the conclusion that can be drawn. For example, "I have seen Tom leaving his house on foot every day, so I know that he walks to work." Whilst it is correct that Tom walks part of the way to work, it is not correct to conclude that he walks all the way to work.

Hasty Generalisation

This is drawing a conclusion based on too little evidence, or too small a sample. Of course, it can often be a matter of opinion about how big a sample is required to draw a conclusion, depending on the mechanics of the issue being addressed.

Contrary Hypothesis

This is where a hypothesis or statement is cannot be consistent with itself. A common example of this is: "If God is omnipotent, can he make a weight that is too heavy for him to lift?" and another is "All truth is relative."

False Dichotomy

If only two options are presented to a problem and then one is discounted by argument this implies that the other path must be followed. The fallacy lies in omitting other alternatives. For example, "You've either got to believe in God or science, and since science is thoroughly researched and peer reviewed no intelligent person will fail to believe in it. Nobody with intelligence can believe in God."

Hypothesis Contrary to Fact

One can look at this as speculation, or sometimes wishful thinking. If "this" hadn't happened then "that" would have happened, or "this" only happened because of "that." For example, "If I'd had a better science teacher I'd have become a scientist." Or "If I'd married someone else then I'd be happier."

Appeal to Authority

This is where we try to get someone to agree with us by claiming that a respected figure has the same opinion as ourselves. Whilst the opinion of a respected authority in a given field is worth serious consideration when discussing their own field, their opinion in a field that is not their own cannot be treated as authoritative. An example might be that of quoting the opinion of a professor of science on matters of theology; their views may be of interest but they are not authoritative.

Begging the Question

Often an argument can be presented that the listener finds that he is comfortable to accept, but with deeper examination he discovers that there is actually no evidence on which to base that acceptance. The argument evades the real question.

Appeal to Ignorance

A fallacy based on the assumption that a statement must be true if it cannot be proved false. This represents a type of false dichotomy in that it excludes other possibilities such as, the statement may be partially true, or unknowable whether it is true. In debates, appeals to ignorance can be used to try shift the burden of proof to the opposing point of view.

Ad Hominem

This fallacy attempts to destroy an argument on the basis of the character of the person who is making it. One might not like the person, or he may have character faults, but that does not mean that the argument itself is incorrect. It is natural not to want to be associated with "unpleasant" people through being seen to hold the same opinion on a particular subject, but we must be careful not to let that sway our opinion.

"No True Scotsman"

The term was coined by Antony Flew, who gave an example of a Scotsman who sees a newspaper article about a series of sex crimes taking place in Brighton, and responds that "no Scotsman would do such a thing." When later confronted with evidence of another Scotsman doing even worse acts, his response is that "no true Scotsman would do such a thing," thus disavowing membership in the group "Scotsman" to the criminal on the basis that the commission of the crime is evidence for not being a Scotsman. However, this is a fallacy as there is nothing in the definition of "Scotsman" which makes such acts impossible. The term "No True Scotsman" has since expanded to refer to anyone who attempts to disown or distance themselves from wayward members of a group by excluding them from it.

Broadly speaking, the fallacy does not apply if there is a clear and well-understood definition of what membership in a group requires and it is that definition which is broken (e.g., "no honest man would lie like that!," "no Christian would worship Satan!" and so on).

Appeal to Pity

The truth of an argument doesn't depend on how people might feel about it, and it is a logical fallacy to try to win support by trying to make the listener feel sorry for someone.

List of Figures

Figure 1: Stereoscopic picture of Blondin crossing Niagara (Robert N. Dennis collection) http://commons.wikimedia.org/wiki/File:Blondin_1860._(Tightrope_artist_%27Blondin%27_crosses_over_the_river.),_from_Robert_N._Dennis_collection_of_stereoscopic_views.jpg

Figure 2: Simulation of the interference of light emerging from two slits

Figure 3: Curvature of space according to the theory of relativity (Source NASA) (http://www.nasa.gov/audience/formedia/features/MP_Photo_Guidelines.html)

Figure 4: Change in the measured speed of light (original artwork)

Figure 5: History of the universe (Credit: NASA / WMAP Science Team http://map.gsfc.nasa.gov/media/020622/index.html)

Figure 6: Composition of the universe and change with time (Credit: NASA / WMAP Science Team http://map.gsfc.nasa.gov/media/080998/index.html)

Figure 7: Effect of different proportions of Dark Matter and energy on the expansion of the universe (http://map.gsfc.nasa.gov/universe/uni_fate.html)

Figure 8: Manufacture of helium in the Sun (http://en.wikipedia.org/wiki/File:FusionintheSun.svg)

Figure 9: Carbon manufacture by the Triple-Alpha Process (http://commons.wikimedia.org/wiki/File:Triple-Alpha_Process.png)

Figure 10: Model of glycine (chemical formula NH2CH2COOH) (http://commons.wikimedia.org/wiki/File:Glycine-3D-balls.png)

Figure 11: Miller-Urey experiment - manufacture of amino acids (http://commons.wikimedia.org/wiki/File:Miller-Urey_experiment-en.svg)

Figure 12: Life cycle of the sun (http://en.wikipedia.org/wiki/File:Solar_Life_Cycle.svg)

Figure 13: Charles Darwin around the time that "Origin of Species" was published (http://commons.wikimedia.org/wiki/File:Charles_Darwin_aged_51.jpg)

Figure 14: Showing how evolution improves fitness (original artwork)

Figure 15: Comparison of Human and Chimpanzee chromosomes (http://commons.wikimedia.org/wiki/File:Humanchimpchromosomes.png)

Figure 16: Lipid molecules in a droplet or bilayer (original artwork)

Figure 17: Diagram of cell membrane with embedded proteins (http://en.mobile.wikipedia.org/wiki/File:Cell_membrane_detailed_diagram_en.svg)

Figure 18: DNA and nitrogenous bases (http://commons.wikimedia.org/wiki/File:DNA_Overview2.png)

Figure 19: Transcription RNA molecule (original artwork)

Figure 20: DNA coiling to form a chromosome (http://upload.wikimedia.org/wikipedia/commons/f/fd/Chromosome_en.svg)

Figure 21: The Window of Perception (original artwork)

Figure 22: Reconstructed London Bridge in Lake Havasu, Arizona. (by Aran Johnson) http://commons.wikimedia.org/wiki/File:London_Bridge,_Lake_Havasu,_Arizona,_2003.jpg

Figure 23: Combination increase with number of variables (original artwork)

Figure 24: Satanic Leaf-Tailed Gecko
(http://commons.wikimedia.org/wiki/File:ALiman_phantasticus.png)

Figure 25: Example of evolutionary convergence
(https://en.wikipedia.org/wiki/File:Armidillidium.vs.glomeris.jpg)

Figure 26: Commonality of passages in the Synoptic gospels
(original artwork)

Figure 27: Rylands fragment P52
(http://commons.wikimedia.org/wiki/File:P52_verso.jpg,
http://commons.wikimedia.org/wiki/File:P52_recto.jpg)

Index

About the Author

Phil Hemsley is a graduate of the University of Cambridge, and a Fellow of the Institution of Mechanical Engineers in the UK. He works for a multinational company in the power industry, has presented technical papers at international conferences and holds many patents. He has lived on both sides of the faith fence. He is married, with two daughters.

6409501R00148

Printed in Great Britain
by Amazon.co.uk, Ltd.,
Marston Gate.